JC 571

THE PARADOXES

OF FREEDOM

The
Paradoxes
of
Freedom

By SIDNEY HOOK

University of California Press

BERKELEY AND LOS ANGELES

1964

UNIVERSITY OF CALIFORNIA PRESS
BERKELEY AND LOS ANGELES
CALIFORNIA

CAMBRIDGE UNIVERSITY PRESS
LONDON, ENGLAND

MANUFACTURED IN THE UNITED STATES OF AMERICA

TO SUSAN

AND

MEHRAN GOULIAN

Preface

This book is an elaboration of three lectures delivered at the University of California, Berkeley, in March, 1961, under the terms of an endowment which provides for an annual series of Jefferson Memorial Lectures. I am grateful to the University of California for the honor bestowed upon me by the invitation to deliver these lectures. I am not only grateful but mindful of the responsibilities it lays upon me to live up to the intellectual obligations of the implied trust of the lectureship.

The lectures were addressed to a general audience, and discuss themes which I hope some day to give more extended and systematic treatment. Clarity is always a boon but sometimes, where matters are complex, it is purchased at too high a price in oversimplification. Since I make no claim to a definitive solution of any problems, but have contented myself with the attempt to state issues clearly and with the presentation of a viewpoint which challenges certain current doctrines, my position may be open to the charge of oversimplification. If I am guilty, my only extenuation can be that the alternative views suffer from far greater oversimplification without possessing any greater validity.

The terms of the lectureship require that the themes discussed have some relation to the broad questions or interests with which Jefferson had some concern. Since Jefferson was not only an eventful and event-making historical figure but a truly encyclopedic mind with a lively curiosity about the science, art, and culture of his time, this gives the lecturer almost carte blanche to take his point of departure from almost any current discipline or fundamental human problem. Partly out of piety to the controversial role Jefferson's thought played in his day, but mainly because of my own interests, I

see Hero in History

have selected certain themes for discussion which are the object of strong disagreement even among those who revere Jefferson's memory.

It is not often that one succeeds in writing a book which on completion promises to please nobody. Although not planned, this, I fear, is such a book. There was a time when I would have defended the views presented in these lectures as a straightforward expression of the liberal American tradition in the broad sense of the phrase. Liberalism was then understood as a commitment to the extension of both civil liberties and social justice and, above all, to the method of pragmatic intelligence as the means of keeping them in a fruitful polar tension. Today the liberal movement has been fragmented into many varieties. There is even a school of totalitarian liberalism—happily not so strong as during the late 'thirties and 'forties—which denies that the enemy ever exists on the "left" but can be found only on the "right," designations which today are more productive of political confusion than of understanding. Some of the differences among these varieties of liberalism are as great as those which divide them from groups commonly regarded as hostile to the entire liberal tradition. Under the circumstances, it is best to avoid labels as much as possible and to explore *problems* in the light of avowed principles and the probable consequences of alternative methods of dealing with them.

Among those who will disagree with much of this book is Milton R. Konvitz, Professor of Law at the New York State School of Industrial and Labor Relations, Cornell University, whose writings and criticisms of the first two chapters have been a source of continuing education to me, and who has done his best—in vain, I fear—to save me from the appearance of amateurishness in discussing constitutional legal questions. However, in relation to the basic questions which concern me most in law, I believe we are all amateurs. The professionals are just as much at odds with each other as the rest of us are. The thinking man in a democracy, to whom these lectures are addressed, must approach these questions with intellectual humility but not with timidity. If he leaves them to the experts to solve, he has surrendered his commitment to democracy.

I am indebted to the Board of Trustees of the Center for Advanced Study in the Behavioral Sciences at Stanford, California, and its director, Dr. Ralph W. Tyler, for the leisure which made it possible for me to rework and expand the original lectures.

S. H.

Contents

1

Intelligence and Human Rights

I HAVE ALWAYS considered myself a Jeffersonian, and came to philosophical maturity under teachers who drew inspiration from his thought. Nonetheless, doubt whether I am really a Jeffersonian arises when I meet other contemporary Jeffersonians or read current works which invoke Jefferson's name and tradition. The writings of Jefferson have acquired a scriptural patina which imparts a pious glow to compositions that artfully quote him in behalf of incompatible positions. Like the Scriptures themselves, his writings bid fair to become all things to all men, and to the devil too.

The struggle over the legacy of Jefferson is an illustration of a familiar phenomenon in the history of ideas. These lectures, however, are not primarily concerned with it. For whatever else that legacy is taken to be, I am confident of two things on which all who regard themselves as Jeffersonians will agree: that the issues Jefferson raised are still of fundamental importance for our life and times; and that they cannot be settled by the argument of authority, whether

the authority be tradition, custom, law, or even the authority of Thomas Jefferson himself. The true Jeffersonian can recognize as supreme only that authority which Jefferson regarded as supreme in human affairs: the authority of human reason.

I

The Virginia Declaration of Rights of 1776 declares that a "frequent recurrence to fundamental principles" is absolutely necessary to preserve the blessings of liberty. This view pays high tribute to the human mind by implying that the preservation of liberty is to some extent dependent upon insight and agreement on its justifications—an essentially philosophical task. It is questionable whether this implication can be sustained if by principles we mean metaphysical presuppositions about the nature of God, man, and their place in the universe. But if by "recurrence to fundamental principles" we mean critical awareness of what we *mean* by freedom, then it seems to me quite true that the future of our freedoms may to some degree depend upon clarification of what is meant by this most ambiguous term.

"Freedom" has always been a fighting word. Today it is an honorific word. Fortunately it has not yet fallen the short distance which separates the honorific from the soporific. The demand for freedom, and for the rights associated with it, is still a clarion cry which wakens us to the presence of something experienced as an abuse. It is a cry which has become universal in the non-Communist world—a cry for national freedom or liberation, social freedom, racial, religious, economic, even linguistic freedom. Whether we turn to Japan or Ceylon, to West Germany, Latin America, or the new African states, we find discussion raging—sometimes not confined to words—over the nature, meaning, implications, limits, and justifications of freedom. In these debates we soon discover that the very same principles are being invoked, amplified, and questioned which agitated the minds of those whom Professor Adrienne Koch has justly denominated the "philosopher-statesmen" of the American Republic.

Nothing confirms more strongly than the contemporary political scene their daring declaration that the principles they formulated were not only a specific response to a local need but also that they possessed a validity which transcended the immediate occasion of their invocation. Their belief, to be sure, was expressed in an archaic idiom and language, but events have vindicated their claim that they had something important and true to say to men everywhere about the nature of just and good government.

The architects of the American Revolution, as distinct from leaders of the French Revolution, made no attempt to carry their plans and blueprints into other countries on bayonet edge. But wherever the news of their Declaration reached, it was understood that the rights of man on which they had staked their lives were rights not only of Englishmen or Americans but of men everywhere. No one could reasonably accuse them of ideological imperialism, even of a liberating kind, because they spread their message solely by force of example rather than by force of arms or by missionary propaganda.

But now a strange thing is observable. The great continuing principle of the American Revolution declares that all governments derive their just powers from the uncoerced consent of the governed. What makes these powers just is that they secure certain rights of men. At the very time when the principle is no longer in dispute anywhere—when even dictatorships must forge a claim that somehow they too rest on consent—in our own country the very concept of human rights, in relation to which legitimate government is defined, has become ambiguous in both formulation and interpretation. The most dramatic expression of the ambiguity and conflict in current interpretations of the nature of human rights is to be found in the opinions of the United States Supreme Court, whose five-to-four decisions exhibit a rapid pendular swing between two incompatible points of view, both of which claim to be rooted in the traditions of the American past.

In this chapter I wish to raise some fundamental questions

3

concerning the nature of human rights, how they are to be conceived and justified. My concern is not primarily historical but analytical—if my analysis is sound, I shall leave to historians the question of how faithful it is to the historical tradition.

What do human rights depend upon? What do we mean when we say that all men have a right to life, liberty, and the pursuit of happiness, or to property in Locke's sense as a general term for "lives, liberties and estates"? Let us leave aside questions of the alleged *origin* of such rights, whether they be traced to God, nature, or some historical compact. What I am asking is the meaning or nature of a "right." It seems clear that whenever we assert that we have a right, whatever else we are asserting, we are asserting or making a claim. If in fact it is a claim to goods or services which society stands ready to enforce, we call it a legal right. But the question we are concerned with is not what is a legal right, not what claims are actually enforced, but what claims *should* be enforced, what *should* be recognized as basic legal rights for all members of the community. As soon as we grasp this distinction, it is obvious that all questions of basic rights involve claims on other persons and therefore are questions of ethics. A right is a claim which entails an obligation or duty on the part of others in specified times and circumstances to recognize it whether in fact the law does so at the moment.

In what does this obligation lie? Theories of obligation are legion. I submit that the least inadequate of them is the view that obligation is derived from the reflective judgment that some shared goal, purpose, or need—some shared interest, want, or feeling—requires the functioning presence of these rights. Without some common nature or some community of feeling, the sense of obligation could hardly develop; the assertion of rights would have no binding or driving emotional force. The demand for rights would be pallid, ungrounded claims. Not even the right of a child to parental care could be sustained in the absence of a sense of identification or commonalty of feeling. Furthermore, without intelligent reflection on the consequences of alternate modes of

4

furthering an actual or presumed common interest, we could not properly choose what claims to raise to the status of rights. Moral rights develop out of the marriage of interests and intelligence. They are nurtured and strengthened by shared interests.

The extent of our rights and obligations is therefore a continuing discovery. Interests come in clusters and hierarchies —some shared, some unshared, and some transformed and modified until shared. At any definite moment the interests which one shares with others constitute a *whole* which exercises some control over the *part*. The interests so modified affect the moving balance of the whole. Just as obviously, the concepts of right and obligation are essentially social notions requiring a community, however small, for their intelligible assertion and recognition. "To ourselves," Jefferson wrote to Thomas Law, "in strict language we can owe no duties, obligation requiring also two parties." [1] That natural rights, as Jefferson understood them, are social in nature is apparent from the fact that he often includes among them the rights to "justice." Although the *meaning* of right and obligation cannot be reduced to the *meaning* of good, the final *justification* of any specific right or obligation must be offered in terms of some shared goods or their anticipated satisfaction.

When these observations are brought to bear on the right to freedom, its moral desirability cannot be determined unless the freedom demanded is specified and considered in a concrete social and historical context. Despite the fact that "freedom" has become a universal rallying cry with strongly emotive associations, a moment's reflection will reveal that no one approves of all kinds of freedom for everyone at all times. When we examine the claims to freedom, even when expressed in the Jeffersonian idiom of natural law, it turns out that they are demands for specific kinds of freedom, usually directed against specific abuses, actual or feared, or obstacles to the fulfillment of specific wants or desires. If challenged, they are ultimately justified by the consequences of denying or granting them.

Jefferson proclaimed that men were endowed with "inherent, inalienable and unchanging rights," and this has been interpreted by some as if their acknowledgment were a precondition of any morally acceptable society. But he also wrote many things which indicate that this is a dubious construction of his meaning. He tells us that he is convinced "that man has no natural right in opposition to his social duties," [2] that "man was destined for society," [3] and that "questions of natural right are triable by their conformity with the moral sense and reason of man. Those who wrote treatises of natural law can only declare what their own moral sense and reason dictate in the several cases they state." [4] Given man's moral sense and reason, the "same act" would be virtuous or vicious, depending, he insists, "on the end it is to effect." [5] What is the end of government? The end or "object of government is to secure the greatest degree of happiness possible to the general mass of those associated under it." [6] Happiness depends "on the circumstances and opinions of different societies," and is a matter of investigation and experiment.

What, then, can guide man's moral sense—which is a social sense—in this welter of relativity? "The answer," he writes, "is that nature has constituted *utility* to man the standard and test of virtue." [7] Quotations of this kind can be multiplied. They indicate, along with a commitment to the moral sense theory, a strong strain of utilitarianism in Jefferson's thought. They suggest that the language of inalienable rights can no more be *literally* construed than the statement "all men are created equal." Just as the natural equality of man was obviously never intended by Jefferson to refer to their physical or psychological traits, but to their "intrinsically moral" equality, as John Dewey puts it,[8] so the so-called natural rights of man are ultimately justified by their personal and social utility in furthering human happiness. In Jefferson—and in Locke before him—nature was identified with reason, the natural and the reasonable were synonymous expressions, and both were logically equivalent to the morally right or justifiable. Natural rights, which it is the function of all just governments to defend, are mythical if

taken literally as preëxistent to society. They are the reasonable, and therefore moral, goals to which all government
action is to be subordinated. Although Locke says, and
Jefferson sometimes implies, that utility is not the ground
but only the consequence of natural rights, both of them
remain inconsistent but wise utilitarians—inconsistent because of the use of expressions like "inalienable," wise because they did not embrace psychological or egoistic hedonism.

This reading of Jefferson, as of Locke, has been denied.
Both have been subjected to devastating critiques by thinkers
who have read them with a nearsighted literalness. One of
them was David Hume, whom Jefferson, enraged at Hume's
Tory bias in his *History of England,* misunderstood and
underestimated and whom he roundly denounces as "a degenerate son of science." There is a passage in Book III of
Hume's *Treatise of Human Nature* (1740) aimed at Locke
which reads like an anticipatory criticism of some of the
expressions of the Declaration of Independence. Criticizing
those who regard promise and consent as "the final obligation
to obedience" to government authority, Hume writes:

All men, say they, are born free and equal; government and
superiority can only be established by consent; the consent of
men, in establishing government, imposes on them a new obligation, unknown to the laws of nature. They, therefore, are bound
to obey their magistrates only because they promise it; and if
they had not given their word, either expressly or tacitly, to preserve allegiance, it would never have become a part of their moral
duty.[9]

After giving some reason for disputing the historical and
psychological adequacy of this account of political obligation,
Hume states his own view as follows:

Government is a mere human invention for the interest of
society. Where the tyranny of the governor removes this interest,
it also removes the natural obligation to obedience. The moral
obligation is founded on the natural, and therefore must cease

where *that* ceases; especially where the subject is such as to make us foresee very many occasions wherein the natural obligation may cease, and causes us to form a kind of general rule for the regulation of our conduct in such occurrences.[10]

Hume is asserting that government derives its justification ultimately from furthering the public interest, and that obligation to obey it ceases whenever it destroys or undermines this interest. Obligation is always a hypothetical, never a categorical, imperative. All this can be restated in terms of Jefferson's doctrine of utility and his belief that governments derive their authority from the consent of the governed, who are presumably the best judges of their own interests.

When we come to Bentham, we can observe how the interpretation of natural rights as purely descriptive expressions or even as *unqualified* normative demands strikes the analytical mind, when it is indifferent to the way in which meaning depends upon historical context. In his *Anarchical Fallacies,* Bentham quotes the proposition from the French Declaration of the Rights of the Man and the Citizen, drawn up under the influence of the American Declaration of Independence: "The end in view of every political association is the preservation of the natural and imprescriptible rights of man. These rights are liberty, property, security and resistance to oppression."

After arguing that rights presuppose the existence of governnment, Bentham comments as follows:

That which has no existence cannot be destroyed—that which cannot be destroyed cannot require anything to preserve it from destruction. *Natural rights* is simple nonsense: natural and imprescriptable rights rhetorical nonsense—nonsense upon stilts. But this rhetorical nonsense ends in the old strain of mischievous nonsense: for immediately a list of these pretended natural rights is given, and those are expressed as to present to view legal rights. And of these rights, whatever they are, there is not, it seems, anyone of which any government can, upon any occasion whatever, abrogate the smallest particle.

So much for terrorist language. What is the language of reason

8

and plain sense upon this same subject? That in proportion as it is *right* or proper, i.e., *advantageous* to the society in question, that this or that right—a right to this or that effect—should be established and maintained, in that same proportion it is *wrong* that it should be abrogated: but that as there is no *right*, which ought not to be maintained so long as it is upon the whole advantageous to the society that it should be maintained, so there is no right which, when the abolition of it is advantageous to society, should not be abolished. To know whether it would be more for the advantage of society that this or that right should be maintained or abolished, the time at which the question about maintaining or abolishing it is proposed, must be given, and the circumstances under which it is proposed to maintain or abolish it; the right itself must be specifically described, not jumbled with an undistinguishable heap of others, under any such vague general terms as property, liberty and the like.[11]

The utilitarian approach has certain difficulties, as we shall see, but two things are significant here. Although in favor of revolution under some circumstances, Bentham was poorly informed about events in America and was no friend of the American Revolution, whose causes he failed to grasp. But he enthusiastically approved of American institutions, and was convinced he could justify the rights of persons or property in terms of his own philosophy. He maintained, with the enchantment that distance and the hope for disciples give, that the grand objective of the American Constitution was "the greatest happiness of the greatest numbers." With some modification, the Jeffersonian principle of utility can do the work which Bentham thought only his formulations can do, but at the sacrifice of the literalness of its language—if it be considered a sacrifice. Bentham was justified in asserting of the French Declaration of the Rights of Man and of a *part* of the Declaration of Independence: "Look to the letter, you find nonsense." He erred in the way great minds sometimes err—greatly—when he added: "Look beyond the letter, you find nothing." [12] For beyond the letter was a generous and moving passion to diminish unnecessary suffering among men and a sense of justice without which even the pursuit of happiness might lend to oppression of individuals and minorities.

We return now to the analysis of the right to liberty or freedom. The logic of Bentham's argument is incontestable. No one can reasonably make a demand for freedom in an unqualified sense—a freedom to do *anything* one pleases. For it is morally impossible to approve all freedoms. If we demand freedom of speech, we cannot justify it merely as a corollary of the demand for freedom as such or of freedom to do whatever one pleases. My demand for freedom to speak is at the same time a demand that the freedom of those who desire to prevent me from speaking should be curbed. When my freedom of speech is a right, it entails the restraining of all restraints on my freedom, the curbing of the freedom of others to curb me. The demand or right to property entails that others be deprived of their freedom to alienate it from me.

"These retrenchments of liberty," says Bentham, "are inevitable. It is impossible to create (or enjoy) rights, to impose obligations, to protect the person, life, private property, subsistence, liberty itself, except at the expense of liberty." [13]

This paradox that "every law is contrary to [someone's] liberty," that no one "can acquire rights except by sacrificing part of his liberty," is denied by some "friends of liberty" who, say Bentham, "are more ardent than enlightened"— the precursors of our own ritualistic liberals to the extent that they overlook the intrinsic conflicts of freedom. They do so by semantic fiat, by abuse and perversion of ordinary linguistic usage. They redefine liberty. They say "liberty consists in the right of doing everything which is not injurious to another," or, as one contemporary philosopher has put it, "freedom is and cannot but be freedom for the good." [14] To which Bentham makes the unanswerable thrust: "But is this the ordinary sense of the word? Is not the liberty to do evil, evil? If not, what is it? Do we not say that it is necessary to take away liberty from idiots and bad men, because they abuse it?" [15]

Failure to recognize that complete freedom in the abstract

covers a multiplicity of undesirable specific freedoms is the source of much confusion. All too often the meaning and associations of the specific historical freedoms won by the American Revolution have become absorbed in the penumbral emotive overtones of the words, which then function as slogans and thus get in the way of clear thought. The term becomes a fetish, and is invoked by groups who want diametrically opposite things.

Because those who invoke freedom want diametrically opposite things, it does not follow that the *meaning* of freedom, in the basic sense of the word when we speak of political freedom, is either contradictory or ambiguous or that we are dealing with incompatible meanings of freedom when one group demands a particular freedom which requires the abridgment of a particular freedom of another group. This no more follows than that the concept of price or money is different for buyers and sellers because the more one gets in a particular transaction the less the other has. This error, forgivable in a statesman making a speech, has misled some political scientists. In an often-quoted speech, Lincoln said in 1864:

The shepherd drives the wolf from the sheep's throat, for which the sheep thanks the shepherd as *liberator,* while the wolf denounces him for the same act as the destroyer of liberty, especially as the sheep was a black one. Plainly the sheep and the wolf are not agreed upon a definition of the word liberty; and precisely the same difference prevails today among us human creatures, even in the North, and all professing to love liberty.

But sheep, wolf, and shepherd do not differ about the *meaning* of liberty—they differ only about which specific liberties are to prevail and for whom. The meaning of liberty common to all is the power to effect one's desires without let or hindrance by others. And the simple point is that no man or creature can effect his desire unless those who attempt to put obstacles in his path or to frustrate his desire are prevented from doing so. And when they are prevented, *their* desire is frustrated.

11

This point is overlooked by one of our leading political scientists, who comments on the above passage from Lincoln as follows:

Political freedom, then, has two different and incompatible meanings according to whether we think of the holder or the subject of political power. Freedom for the holder of political power signifies the opportunity to exercise political domination; freedom for the subject means the absence of such domination. Not only are these two conceptions of freedom mutually exclusive in logic, but they are also incapable of existing in fact with any particular sphere of action. One can only be realized at the expense of the other, and the more there is of one, the less there is bound to be of the other.[16]

There is only one *concept* of freedom involved here: what is incompatible in fact is the mutual exercise of freedom on the part of both ruler and subject. In giving freedom to the one we must deny it to the other. There are some freedoms of which this is not true: the freedom of a person to read or study does not require the abridgment of someone else's freedom to read or study; it requires only the denial of freedom to those who would prevent him from reading or studying. As well argue that because the more money distributed in dividends, the less money remains for distribution in wages, proves we are dealing with two different *concepts* of money as to argue that because the more freedom a government has to act, the less freedom is possessed by those whose actions it affects, proves we are confronted by two different concepts of freedom.

An analysis of the nature of money cannot be a guide to what we should spend our money for. We may disagree about the proper analysis of the function of money, once we have identified in an appropriate way what we mean by money, and agree about what it should be spent for. And, conversely, we may agree on the proper analysis of the function of money and disagree about how we should spend it.

Analogously, whatever our formal analysis of the concept of freedom, this by itself cannot determine which freedoms to approve, which to disapprove. We may agree on the formal analysis of freedom but, assuming that the term is being used in a common sense (otherwise we are talking past each other about two different things and neither agreeing nor disagreeing), we may still disagree as bitterly as sheep and wolf as to who is to enjoy his freedom. Conversely, we may disagree on the formal analysis of freedom and yet agree on what freedoms should be encouraged or not. What we must avoid in the interest of clarity is to make the freedoms we believe men *should* enjoy part of the very meaning of the term, because those who disagree with our list of preferred freedoms may do the same. When this happens, the issues get bogged down in a semantic swamp. When dispute breaks out over what freedom *really* means, it is usually not a dispute over the meaning of freedom in actual use but over differences concerning what specific freedoms should be granted or curbed.

Freedom does not mean the same thing as virtue or goodness. Freedom is not wisdom. Nor truth nor beauty nor any other desirable thing, although many desirable things presuppose the existence of freedom. There are freedoms and freedoms—and we cannot have them all. For each one we must pay a price. All choice of freedoms commits us ultimately to an ethical position. The gratification of any desire as such may be abstractly desirable but so long as there are desires which seek to frustrate other desires, choice among them is inescapable.

The logical correlative, so to speak, of a particular freedom espoused is the negation of the freedom to frustrate it. We know this without empirical inquiry, from an analysis of the very meaning of a serious claim to that freedom. But we soon discover as an empirical fact in this world that freedoms conflict existentially. We want more than one freedom, and we then find out that, as the world is constituted, the fulfillment of the one leads to the frustration of the other. It is this failure to realize that any specific freedom which we regard as desirable is only one among a plurality of other desirable freedoms, proclaimed as rights, which is responsible for the absolutistic interpretation of the rights enumerated in the Declaration of Independence and the Constitution, especially of its Bill of Rights. I, for one, have never been able to bring myself to believe that the philosopher-statesmen of the American Republic were absolutists, despite some high judicial authority which endorses this view. Grant, for the moment, even on the absolutistic view, that men are endowed with inalienable rights to life, liberty, pursuit of happiness, and property—and the indefinite number of other rights which these generic terms encompass. Surely no one could be so optimistic as to believe that they are all and always compatible with each other. The right to liberty, however specified, sometimes threatens the right to property and vice versa, and either or both of them may on occasion conflict with the right to the pursuit of happiness. Sometimes a community concludes that the right to political liberty or the right to justice is "more precious than life itself" and goes down fighting. Indeed if it never did, and it opted for survival at any price in any circumstance, such survival would be a perpetual badge of infamy. At any rate, no matter how the conflict between rights be resolved, one or the other right must be alienable. Otherwise the inalienable would entail the unlimited. If one denies unlimited powers to government, this does not entail the recognition of any unlimited specific right of the governed.

As against this view, which denies that inalienable means absolute, Justice Black has recently declared: "It is my belief that there *are* 'absolutes' in our Bill of Rights, and that they were put there on purpose by men who knew what the words meant, and meant their prohibitions to be 'absolutes' . . ." [17] In answer to the question whether "liberties *admittedly* covered by the Bill of Rights can nevertheless be abridged on the ground that a superior public interest justified the abridgment," he replies in many rhetorical variations with a thunderous NO.

Nor is Justice Black alone in his belief. Not only are some of his judicial brethren sympathetic to his point of view, some American scholars, legal as well as philosophical, have

also endorsed it. It is at the basis of the critical evaluation
and rejection in some influential quarters of the Holmesian
doctrine of "clear and present danger," as a justifiable limitation on freedom of speech, press, and assembly. Here is a
typical pronouncement by Alexander Meiklejohn:

> No one who reads with care the text of the First Amendment
> can fail to be startled by the absoluteness. The phrase "Congress
> shall make no law . . . abridging the freedom of speech," is un-
> qualified. It admits of no exceptions . . . under any circum-
> stances . . . they established an absolute, unqualified prohibi-
> tion of the abridgment of the freedom of speech.[18]

It is my view that this interpretation of Jefferson—indeed,
its protagonists do not put it forward as an interpretation
but as an incontestable fact—misreads Jefferson, who sparked
the movement for the adoption of the Bill of Rights.
Whether or not it misreads Jefferson, this interpretation is
wrong—disastrously wrong. I believe it misreads Jefferson
because the checks Jefferson placed on government were
moral not metaphysical absolutes. "The will of the majority
must be rightful," he declared in his First Inaugural, "but,
to be rightful it must be reasonable," he added. And to be
reasonable is to be absolute about nothing except about being
reasonable.

Before discussing this view of absolute rights as a proposition in constitutional law, let us look at it candidly as a
proposition in ethics. To be sure there is a difference between
politics and ethics, but if we believe with Jefferson that they
are related where fundamental questions are involved, then
whatever is discovered to be morally right should not be
politically wrong even though it may not be politically necessary. In morals is there any concrete value or right which
one can define as unconditionally or absolutely valid in all
circumstances? Take any natural or moral good, like strength
or beauty, friendship or loyalty, love or truth. Would any
reasonable person be prepared to say that it must be pursued
in all circumstances and never be abridged or sacrificed?
Even for Kant, the most rigorous of all moralists, nothing

can be absolutely good except the good will, because without the good will all natural and moral goods may be abused. But the presence of good will can be determined only by formal considerations and hence can be no guide to action. Nicolai Hartmann recognizes that every good has a critical point or *Umschlag* beyond which, if it is pursued, it becomes evil. Courage becomes foolhardiness; caution cowardice; love of beauty or knowledge an abomination, when it leads to the practice and enjoyment of torture. Sir David Ross is not a utilitarian, but for him rights and duties are always prima facie: they may conflict with other rights and duties, so that my prima facie duty to tell the truth and my prima facie duty to be kind may conflict, making it necessary for me to sacrifice one or the other. Let us grant for the moment the right, as unqualified as you please, to speak our minds and express the truth as we see it. Let us grant, as another unqualified right, the right to a fair trial. If freedom of speech, as it sometimes does, prejudices or imperils a man's right to a fair trial (not to speak of cases when it threatens a man's right to life—for example, when a mob is being incited to a lynching), how can *both* be absolute or unqualified? What happens when the right to property conflicts with the right to safety, the right to education, the right to defense (and the complex cluster of rights implied in the very preamble of the Constitution)? When freedom of press grievously violates the right to privacy, which is to yield to which and under what conditions? The right to tax is not necessarily a power to destroy, but it certainly is a power to abridge property and redistribute wealth. In morals, one good or right limits another: can it be any different in political life or in any intelligent construction of constitutional law?

Further, I have argued that morality is essentially social. Every act is caught up in the web of human association which constitutes culture, in the continuing processes of meaningful interaction in time which constitute human history. The very quality of a moral act—whether of obligation or duty—depends upon, among other things, its effects on the community in which we are nurtured. Who then can seriously contend, except on the basis of a supernatural morality, that the entire moral quality of any act can be assessed independently of its consequences upon the good of a society— present or future? Who but a fanatic can say: "I have a right to do this or that independently of *any* consequence, of any weal or woe for my fellows"? What mere man can claim that he has the omniscience which would justify him in asserting that no conceivable circumstance could ever arise, no possible effects could ever ensue, which would be a reasonable ground for limiting an action he proclaims as his natural and absolute right? The disinterested pursuit of knowledge is among the noblest and most beneficial of human ideals. But the experimenter who practices vivisection on a human being against his will is the stock illustration of a madman or a moral monster. Were effective disarmament controls to be introduced in the world, it might be necessary in the interests of international peace to forbid certain types of experimental research, even if only temporarily. There are times when even a joke about planting a bomb on an airplane is an antisocial act punishable by sanctions—because we cannot risk the situation in which a true warning is dismissed as another joke!

As we shall see, there are certain difficulties in this position —no moral position is free of difficulties—but they are not so grave as the difficulties in any absolutist position, because the latter are morally insuperable. Since conflict between alleged absolutes is inescapable, we seek intelligent compromise or resolution at the risk of being charged with opportunism or cowardly evasion by those who assume that an inflexible backbone must be the sheath of intelligence.

Before discussing this, however, let us further consider Jefferson's position and the history of the Bill of Rights in the light of the absolutist interpretation.

Did Jefferson believe that any rights were absolute? He was much too intelligent. "There are extreme cases," he once wrote, "where the laws become inadequate even to their own preservation. . . ." In a letter to J. B. Colvin he develops this idea:

A strict observance of the written laws is doubtless *one* of the high duties of a good citizen, but it is not *the highest*. The laws of necessity, of self-preservation, of saving our country when in danger, are of higher obligation. To lose our country by a scrupulous adherence to written law, would be to lose the law itself, with life, liberty, property and all those who are enjoying them with us: thus absurdly sacrificing the end to the means . . . A ship at sea in distress for provisions, meets another having abundance, yet refusing a supply; the law of self-preservation authorizes the distressed to take a supply by force. In all these cases, the unwritten laws of necessity, of self-preservation, and of the public safety, control the written laws of *meum* and *tuum*.[19]

There is no more of a formal contradiction in this than in the fact that a man who believes in peace must sometimes fight for it. He must fight for it not only because the enemy will not let him live in peace but because, like Jefferson, he is committed to plural values—to peace, to be sure, but also to political freedom *and* to the ideal of a self-governing republic. Nor is Jefferson saying that the public safety is the highest good, the altar on which all values must be sacrificed. Our moral predicaments flow from the conflicts among our ideals; our moral intelligence consists in resolving them by the discovery of that alternative which best promises to strengthen the entire structure of our remaining values. Needless to say, we pay a price for any alternative, even for the best. The price in the concrete situation is always the sacrifice or abridgment of some right or good which politically innocent minds fancy absolute.

A curious defense has recently been made of Justice Black's position by Professor Charles L. Black of the Yale Law School.[20] According to this defense, Justice Black is clearly wrong in contending that any right is absolute. Taken literally, it is admitted, Justice Black's position is untenable. But he must not be taken literally or even cognitively. His words, sensibly understood, must be construed as an expression of an "attitude." It means that in the pinches and crises the absolutist stands firm and unmoved as a rock as the waters of opinion, doubt, and reflection wash over him. The non-absolutist, on the other hand, is likely to be a trimmer or an opportunist who under the pretext of social policy abandons the threatened value. Absolutists are therefore to be trusted to fight the good fight for an imperiled, precious freedom to the bitter end. The plain implication is that the non-absolutist, sure of nothing except that the problem of choice is hard, cannot be loyal to any treasured right.

The weakness of this defense is that it abandons the quest for rational decision at the very point where inquiry is most needed. Attitudes are of course always involved in value judgments or commitments, but they do not solve problems. The great problems and crucial pinch of issues arise, as we have seen, not when a prima facie right confronts a prima facie wrong, but when a prima facie right conflicts with a prima facie right, as in the Japanese relocation cases, in which the prima facie right of national security was counterposed to the prima facie right of our Japanese fellow citizens to the possession of their homes and freedom, and, on the evidence of the objective risks involved, was wrongly decided by the very court on which Justice Black sat and justified by an opinion he himself wrote.[21]

When attitude confronts attitude in a real problem, how is the shock of conflicting attitudes to be mediated except through the process of inquiry? The process of inquiry is short-circuited when, in advance of deliberation, a particular value or attitude is taken as so sacred as to be beyond reflective criticism and possible rejection in the light of the relevant circumstances. Most problems which require decision are easily settled in the light of cumulative historical experience, but we are here concerned with the hard cases fashioned by genuinely problematic situations.

Insofar as psychological and historical evidence about attitudes is relevant, it shows that the stronger the attitude of absolutism, the more likely is it to be associated with fanaticism, intolerance, and reckless disregard of the consequences and costs of action. John Brown is a case in point. Absolutism as an attitude in history has about it the aura of fagots and stake rather than of the compassion and vision which sees the human being even in an enemy. By its mood of self-righteousness it paralyzes the attempt to find solutions to problems by the use of creative intelligence in resolving conflicts. *Logically* it is possible for one who believes he has the absolute truth to tolerate error. But *psychologically* the absolute conviction that one has the absolute truth about human affairs is almost always the tell-tale sign of the persecutor.

I say "almost always" because historically there have been a few occasions in which absolutists have been the innocent victims of other absolutists, like Sir Thomas More, who was a martyr to the absolutism of Henry VIII. The content of an absolutist's belief may be as inoffensive as a dietary taboo. But were this belief to have consequences that affected the health and life of others, the effects might hardly be distinguishable from acts of persecution. A vegetarian who refused to allow his child to take nourishment or medicine essential to preserving his life, on the ground that it breached an inviolable commandment, would differ only in psychological degree from a crusading absolutist. Even a person who made an absolute of tolerance would, on pain of foolishness, have to draw the line at tolerating the actively intolerant in circumstances in which such tolerance resulted in great evil otherwise avoidable. From the standpoint of a humanist morality, as distinct from transcendental religion, the same would be true if one were to act on the absolutism of love. Those who say they love Hitler and Stalin and would punish only their actions are using the term "love" in a special sense. The presence of love is normally manifested in loving action. Whoever acts lovingly when the consequences of such action can be correctly foreseen to lead to evils that could have been avoided by non-loving behavior, without producing evils of equal or worse magnitude, is morally co-responsible for the resulting situation.

At any rate to suggest, even by indirection, that conflicting attitudes toward the doctrine of absolute rights reflect, on the part of absolutists, a staunch defense of the Bill of Rights "without regard to transient legislative views on the pressing necessity of shutting people up" but, on the part of the non-absolutists, a truckling to such legislative views, seems singularly inept if tested by the attitudes evinced by the justices of the Supreme Court to issues arising from the Bill of Rights. Neither Holmes nor Brandeis, neither Cardozo nor Frankfurter, took the theory of absolute rights seriously. Yet some of their most powerful opinions—sometimes in dissent, sometimes not—were written in defense of civil rights. Nor is it wrong to "regard" with respect legislative views, which are always transient, any more than it would be to "regard" with respect the views of justices, which are also transient. To "regard" does not necessarily mean to follow blindly. Unless one believes in one's infallibility, the wise decision is more likely to result from regarding than from disregarding the views of a coördinate branch of government.

It is sometimes recognized that there is a certain ambiguity in the concept of absolute. In one sense the meaning of "absolute" is innocuous and irrelevant to the issue under inquiry. To the extent that any rule is clearly and unambiguously expressed, it is insofar forth absolute in meaning and application. Exceptions, where stated or allowed, become part of the rule which is no less absolute because it states the special case when the general rule no longer applies or may be modified. Among the differences between legal laws, considered as rules, and the rules of chess or spelling is that, among the latter, conflict between rules represents intellectual incoherence—the game cannot be properly played, the word cannot be properly spelled, unless there is a higher-order rule which resolves the apparent conflict of rules. A new game might result or a new canon of spelling. But in law, conflict of rights and duties confronts us on all sides. Almost every case brought to court illustrates it. Where a rule is laid down that under such and such circumstances if certain rights clash, one of them shall prevail, does not this decision, one may ask, also express an absolute right *under these specified circumstances* as much as rules of spelling or chess? The answer, it seems to me, is that the right favored or expressed by the rule which guides conflicts between prima facie rights is not absolute except conditionally— that is, it is merely more definite and precise in the set of given conditions. It guides us in deciding the class of cases created by similar conflicts of rights in similar conditions. It does not necessarily bind us forever. If by "absolute," we mean unchanging and unchangeable, then we may say that only if the sum total of relevant circumstances and presuppositions recur could the value expressed by the decision be taken as absolute. But the very nature of social and historical life is that the relevant circumstances and presuppositions may change. Circumstances and presuppositions do not, of course, always change, nor when they do, do they change relevantly. But here the readiness is all—the open-minded-ness to new considerations, the receptivity to fresh, emergent interests, the awareness of new horizons of knowledge as they bear on issues—all these, but of course not only these, must enter into the specific decision.

Let us test the claim to the absolute character of the rights expressed in the Bill of Rights by a closer glance at the provisions of the First Amendment.

II

The text of the First Amendment contains more than reference to freedom of speech, press, and assembly. It asserts also that "Congress shall make no law respecting an establishment of a religion, or prohibiting the free exercise thereof." The language is palpably as "definite" and "unequivocal" as that which prohibits abridgments of freedom of speech, press, and assembly. I shall not discuss freedom of worship as a natural right, but as a moral right and as a claim to be absolute, unqualified, and inalienable. Despite Justice Black, it is obvious that the authors of these words about religious freedom could not have possibly intended that the exercise of *any* religion cannot be abridged, for if it could never be abridged, anything commanded by any religion would be legally permitted, which, in view of the varieties of religion that have flourished in this world, has never been, is not, never will be, nor should be the case.

The question of religion is very interesting. Notice that there is no distinction made here between the free exercise of religious thought and the free exercise of religious practice. It would be absurd to say that men have an absolute right to worship God according to their conscience only so long as they do not act on it, so long as they keep their religious thought to themselves. It would be absurd, because as all anthropologists and scholars of comparative religion know, religion is essentially related to ritual and ceremonial practices. It is an integrated system of beliefs and practices related to things deemed sacred. In all institutional religions, behavior—and not thought alone—counts. The good Christian, Jew, or Muslim is known by his practices. It would mock anybody who lived according to his religion to assure him that he has an absolute right to worship God in his thought but not in the actions or practices which reflect that thought. And it is as a mockery that we sense today the reply which Oliver Cromwell made to a besieged Catholic community in Ireland which offered to surrender on the sole condition of being permitted to exercise freedom of conscience: "As to freedom of conscience, I meddle with no man's conscience; but if you mean by that, liberty to celebrate the Mass, I would have you understand that in no place where the power of the Parliament of England prevails shall that be permitted." [22] Today, despite the record of flagrant religious oppression in the Soviet Union, Russian Communists insist that there is a sharp distinction between religious *thought* and religious *practice,* and claim that they guarantee the former. This hypocrisy fools no one.

No one with knowledge of the wide and extreme practices covered by the term religion could have meant that human beings have a right, no less an absolute right, to practice *any* religion. Religious freedom is, has been, and should be always subject to the control of ethical principles. It is these which have primacy. Under our Bill of Rights, which guarantees freedom of religion, we do not permit a religion of human sacrifice or mutilation; we do not tolerate the refusal to pay taxes on religious grounds; we do not permit parents on religious grounds to prevent their children from being inoculated against disease or from receiving an education. We do not even permit otherwise law-abiding citizens piously to carry out the command of the Old Testament to be fruitful and multiply through a system of plural marriages.[23] It would be adding insult to injury to tell Mormons that their freedom to exercise their religion was really not being restricted, because they could still believe in the desirability of polygamy even as they sat in jail as a consequence of practicing it. *it was done*

The example of religion is not only interesting but decisive for the purposes of the analysis. Freedom to worship God according to one's conscience is the first, the oldest, the most fiercely fought for freedom in the history of human thought. Most religious groups in history have cared little about freedom of speech, press, and assembly save in religious matters, and have been cheerfully prepared to sacrifice freedom in secular affairs if it were a condition precedent for the unrestricted exercise of their own religion. What they desired, as Figgis trenchantly puts it, "was not liberty or tolerance, but domination and independence." [24] The first was the unintended consequence of failure to achieve the second. "Political liberty is the residuary legatee of ecclessiastical animosities"—animosities which flowed from competing fanaticisms. But no matter how fanatical a religionist may be, he must acknowledge that some religious freedom is subject to moral check—although it is the other man's religion he wants to check. He will always claim a moral sanction for his own religious practices, even if it be the practice of suttee.

The moral ideals of a community change of course, but the principle of moral control does not. If the community were to become convinced that it is morally wrong to impose unnecessary suffering on animals, it could legitimately restrict certain types of ritual slaughter even if in so doing it would run counter to the religious taboos of some religious groups. Conversely, if as a result of a permanent imbalance between the number of men and women in the population, we changed our mind about the morality or immorality of plural marriages, we might then not be justified in abridging the free exercise of the traditional Mormon religion.

What seems to be clear about one provision of the First Amendment—that respecting the free exercise of religion—is interpreted as a wild paradox when applied to its other provisions, especially freedom of speech. Here with warning finger and in sepulchral tones which proclaim the imminent death of the Republic, Justice Black tells us that the record permits no comparable interpretation, for the language forsooth "is composed of plain words easily understood," words that are "positive," "absolute," "emphatic." [25] One wonders how, then, there *could* be any dispute about its meaning; and how the justices of the Supreme Court could be locked in *prolonged* conflict over the scope and implications of the provisions of the First Amendment.

The answer is that all words are subject to interpretation in the light of their contexts and presuppositions and in the light of their implications, which, because they are infinite, can never be completely grasped at any one moment. The absolutists, despite themselves, interpret too. They interpret the word "abridge" in such a way that they coolly tell a man who is being punished for polygamous religious practice that his religious freedom is *not* being abridged. This seems to me bad interpretation. Were one to proceed in the same way where speech is concerned, a man could be muzzled for the most innocuous remark and assured that he was still talking.

Indeed, as we have already seen, the very meaning of the word "absolute" must be interpreted. The adjective "absolute" has many different meanings, but when Justice Black speaks of an "absolute" right he means a power or obligation or duty that is "inviolable," "unlimited," "unconditional," "inalienable" in any circumstance "however great this nation's emergency and peril may be," [26] to use his own phrase. On this view, as we have seen, there simply cannot be two absolute rights if they can conceivably conflict. And who can guarantee that any two rights conceived absolutely will never conflict? Since the Bill of Rights, as well as the main body of the Constitution, enumerates many rights, it is obvious that they cannot all be absolute.

There is another interpretation of "absolute," to which absolutists sometimes revert, that would make any limitation or extension of a right absolute. The Fifth Amendment states, among other things, that no one "shall be compelled in any *criminal* case to be a witness against himself, nor be deprived of life, liberty or property without *due process of law;* nor shall private property be taken for public use without *just* compensation." All these rights are considered absolute too. But what do the expressions here italicized—*criminal, due process of law,* and *just*—mean? The extension of the meaning of "criminal case" with respect to the privilege against self-incrimination is notorious; "due process of law" is even more ambiguous; and the word "just" is most ambiguous. Every extended interpretation of these expressions apparently generates a series of absolute rights. Speaking of "due process of law," Justice Black says: "Whatever [sic!] its meaning, however, then there can be no doubt that it must be granted." [27]

Does this mean that public utility corporations have an *absolute* right to earnings of more than 7 per cent because state legislation regulating the limit of their return on investment was once declared unconstitutional on the ground that it deprived a corporation of property without due process of law? If absolute rights are to be made and unmade by judges, what is to prevent a judge from ruling that a vote of thanks and a bronze medal are *just* compensation for the confiscation of property? After all, the Constitution does not define "justice."

The main contention of absolutists is that the rights enumerated in the Bill of Rights and the other articles of the Constitution are "so absolute a command that Congress is wholly without authority to violate it, however great this nation's emergency and peril may be." If this is so, then those who drew up the American Constitution must have been incoherent. For Section IX provides that "the privilege of the Writ of Habeas Corpus" shall be suspended "when in cases of rebellion or invasion the public safety may require it." It is obvious that all the rights and privileges of the Bill of Rights become nugatory when the writ of habeas corpus is suspended.

To retort to this that the Constitution specifies the conditions under which the writ of habeas corpus shall be suspended is not germane to the point I am making. The point is that the Constitution itself recognizes explicitly not only that circumstances may make all constitutional guarantees irrelevant but implicitly that there are potential conflicts among the ideals, rights, and privileges it enumerates, and that therefore none is absolute and all must be intelligently interpreted—in the one instance of extreme danger to national survival, and in every instance when they seriously conflict. Who shall interpet them is another question to be discussed later. But all intelligent interpretation takes us away from hypnotic fixation on the text (although the text is of course to be considered) to the purposes and ideals of the Constitution and to the legitimate needs of contemporary democratic society. For example, suppose there existed incontrovertible evidence that an enemy power using modern intercontinental missiles was planning to destroy the country *without* invasion. If the public safety required that the writ of habeas corpus be suspended, how would we regard the objection that such suspension is unconstitutional, on the ground that the Constitution defines in absolute terms the condition for suspension as one of "invasion"? (Of course, we could *redefine* invasion to cover cases which are not cases of invasion as ordinarily understood. Were we to do this, it would be tantamount to abandoning the doctrine of absolute rights).

It is safe to say in answer to the question that such an objection would appear to reflective judgment to be just as much in defiance of common sense as Justice Black's reading of the Fifth Amendment. He explicitly tells us that the injunction in the Fifth Amendment against confiscation of property without just compensation must be considered absolutely valid and binding even if the safety and survival of the country depended upon its being suspended, as in extreme cases they very well might. Justice Black is, however, not unreasonable. If the danger were very great, he tells us we can amend the Constitution. The enemy or the danger presumably would oblige by waiting for the constitutional process of amendment to run its course. "My reason for refusing this approach [to balance conflicting rights] would be that I think the Fifth Amendment's command is absolute and not to be overcome without constitutional amendment even in times of grave emergency." [28]

To deny the right of a duly constituted democratic government to confiscate property without just compensation in any possible situation—no matter how extreme, no matter at what cost in human life (something which should be more important to us than property), and no matter whether the survival of the nation was at stake—is doctrinaire. It is not necessary to go so far in order to recognize as a firm general rule that government is forbidden to take or destroy property without just compensation. It may be compared to a rule or commandment against violence which every humane person knows we may have to violate in an extreme circumstance in order to save a human life. As we have seen, nothing is so stark a fact in human experience as the conflict of rights. If we refuse to think about rights when they conflict, we may be compelled to think about them in determining how to interpret key phrases like "just," "due process," or "cruel and unusual punishment." A good argument can be made for the contention that the Eighteenth Amendment in effect expropriated the property of American brewers without just compensation. So did Lincoln's Proclamation of Emancipation before the Fourteenth Amendment was adopted. Had a Southern slaveholder brought an action against the federal government on the ground that Lincoln's action violated his absolute right under the Fifth Amendment not to have his property confiscated without just compensation, he could have used Justice Black's formulation quite aptly. One might of course dispute Lincoln's assumption that the preservation of the Union required the Proclamation of Emancipation. But even if there were no question whatsoever that the preservation of the Union did require it, on Justice Black's contention it would have to be condemned. Similarly most rent control laws, which prevent landlords from receiving the income they would normally earn where housing resources are scarce, would have to be condemned out of hand, on Justice Black's position. For no matter what ethical or legal or political justification we offer for these rent control laws, there is an element of confiscation of income in them which clearly violates the absolutist interpretation of the Fifth Amendment. The same is true of the power of the state to declare that places where liquor is manufactured or sold are common nuisances and to order forfeiture of their property,[29] or to decree the destruction of cedar trees, without compensation, in order to protect apple orchards from cedar rust.[30]

Modern logicians are paying increasing attention to the logic of presupposition. The attention is as needful as it is belated, not only to remove certain paradoxes, but also because the intelligibility of ordinary discourse often depends upon implicit and unspoken presuppositions which, if ignored, rob assertions of their point or make them sound impossibly extreme. A great deal was presupposed by the statements of the framers of the Constitution. They were so familiar with the context and historical-things-taken-for-granted of their words that they no more thought it necessary to state them than we do with respect to many of our current expressions. These historical presuppositions can be inferred from the study of the related documents and writings of the times together with the accepted practices. Such studies bear only on the meanings that the words had *at the time* to those who employed them. These meanings are not necessarily prescriptive for us, although we should all like to believe that our own meanings are continuous with those of the great men whose liberal heritage we are developing. The meanings of words examined in the light of their historical presuppositions are not prescriptive for us, because in the end we ourselves must take the responsibility for preserving the meanings the framers of the Constitution gave their words and extending or abandoning them. The question "What meaning *should* we give these key words?" is morally prior to "What meaning did they give them?" The second question is logically independent of the first. It is a question of historical truth.

What were the historical presuppositions of the freedoms of the First Amendment? At the time the Bill of Rights was adopted is there any evidence to believe that the practice among the states, or the dominant opinions of the framers, interpreted the freedoms of the First Amendment along the lines currently taken by Justices Black and Douglas? Directly and indirectly, the latter have claimed that they are the heirs of the libertarian traditions of the founders of the American Republic, and that those who have disagreed with them have renounced this tradition. They have not offered their interpretation of the First Amendment merely as a *proposal* that we read it in such a way that it functions as a bar upon any regulation or restriction of "absolute" freedom of speech. They have not contented themselves with justifying their proposal in terms of our commitment to the logic, ethics, and politics of the democratic process. They have flatly asserted again and again that in fact their interpretation coincides with the incontrovertible historical record. They are almost as absolute in their historical claims as in their juridical claims that the practices of the states and the dominant doctrine of the founders of the American Republic, at the time the Constitution was adopted, countenanced no regulation "within reasonable limits" of freedom of speech, press, and assembly.

Unfortunately for their position, the historical evidence is overwhelmingly against them. They are even wrong in their categorical assertion that "the First Amendment repudiated seditious libel for this country." [31] They have confused the almost universal opposition to the doctrine of *prior restraint* on utterances, or censorship *in advance* of publication, with the view that individuals have a right to express their opinions, true or false, regardless of who or what is affected by their expression—a view which was almost universally rejected at the time, much as we may deplore that rejection. Freedom of speech and press in the light of existing practices meant the right to speak and publish without prior restraint or censorship or licensing. It did *not* mean the right to do so with impunity. It did *not* mean the right to legal protection against seditious or criminal libel. That the meaning of freedom was understood in this restricted sense at the time, I repeat, need not bind us and has not bound us. But fidelity to fact should compel us to recognize that, unfortunately, the way the Daughters of the American Revolution and kindred organizations today interpret the First Amendment is much closer to how the makers of the American Revolution actually understood it in *their* time than the way civil libertarians of most schools of thought do today, absolutist or not. This observation is a greater tribute to the piety of such organizations than to their intelligent loyalty to the spirit of an open society. It is no reflection upon the liberal thought and practice of the eighteenth century in the context of the historical struggle for extending the sphere of political rights.

The reader who wishes to examine the evidence will find it in a recent work whose findings are all the more impressive because they are so philosophically unpalatable to its author.[32]

So much for the historical presuppositions of the language of the Bill of Rights. Since Justice Black sets such great store on the language of the founders and on the historical record to justify his view that the Bill of Rights expresses "absolute commands" against even reasonable restrictions or regulations of speech, his historical errors should constitute formidable difficulties for him. They should also be of some concern to the community because of his further contention that the "Courts have neither the right nor the power to review the original decision of the Framers. . . ." [33]

It is of course not necessary to make the meaning of the

Bill of Rights depend upon narrow historical presuppositions. There are, in addition, what we may call "common sense presuppositions." By this phrase I mean the understanding which is implicitly involved when a common task is undertaken to achieve a common goal in determinate situations. Common-sense presuppositions are never completely free from historical ones, since common sense too has a history in that its judgments are confirmed by experience. But they are distinguishable from specific historical assumptions by their presence in classes or families of situations whose members have different histories. Among the obvious common-sense presuppositions of the words used in the First Amendment was that the outlawing of legislation against freedom of speech did not immunize individuals from legal penalties incurred by slanderous and/or libelous communications which had consequences of extreme gravity to those slandered or libeled. This has been explicitly acknowledged by the Court.[34]

Some such presupposition seems a prerequisite for almost any ordered society of a certain degree of complexity. The social interest in recognizing laws of this character follows from the fact that without them a community would be in perpetual turmoil rent by feuds, assault, riot, and even lynch law. Roscoe Pound has persuasively argued that a man has not only a legitimate personal interest which may be injured by libel and slander but also a legitimate personal interest, a "claim to be secured in his dignity and honor as part of his personality," [35] a point which becomes clear when we recall our normal reactions to words which cast unjust aspersions upon the honor of a woman.

Although Jefferson's language is sometimes cited as if he denied these common-sense presuppositions, we know from the very letters in which he urged the adoption of a Bill of Rights that he assumed them. Thus writing to Madison, he observes: "A declaration, that the federal government will never restrain the presses from printing anything they please, will not take away the liability of printers for false facts printed. The declaration, that religious faith shall be unpunished, does not give impunity to criminal acts, dictated by religious error." [36]

Another common-sense presupposition of the words of the First Amendment is that in the context of ordinary discourse the prohibition on legislation restricting free speech would not bar punishing a person whose speech or published words clearly counseled or advised the commission of a criminal act. Morally, if an act is wrong it is morally wrong to encourage someone to perform it, even though the degree of blame or unworthiness may not be the same for advising the commission of a wrong as for committing it. If the morally wrong act is also legally punishable, then the morally wrong act of encouragement is in principle also punishable. It is in effect abetting the act. "Must I shoot a simple soldier boy who deserts," Lincoln once asked, "while I must not touch a hair of a wily agitator who induces him to desert?" If there is no reasonable doubt about the facts, the question answers itself.

It seems to me that it was this common-sense presupposition to which Justice Holmes was alluding, and not so much to the historical presupposition, when he wrote:

The First Amendment while prohibiting legislation against free speech as such cannot have been, and obviously was not, intended to give immunity for every possible use of language . . . We venture to believe that neither Hamilton nor Madison nor any other competent person, *then or later,* ever supposed that to make criminal the counseling of a murder within the jurisdiction of Congress would be an unconstitutional interference with free speech.[37]

Common-sense presuppositions are at the basis of Holmes's original formulation of the "clear and present danger" doctrine as limiting the freedoms of the First Amendment. That the character of an act depends upon circumstances; that speech itself may be an act; that intent is relevant in assessing the meaning of an action; that we are justified in holding normal people to account for the normal consequences of an action which past experience has shown highly injurious, even if they intended only the action but not the consequences; that an unsuccessful crime is still a crime, although sometimes not equally punishable—all these assumptions and many others are common-sense presuppositions out of which the doctrine arose. The formulation of the doctrine is beset with incurable ambiguity if these presuppositions are disregarded. When do words create a *clear* danger and to whom? Does *present* danger refer to the specious moment or to a slab of time—a day, month, year, decade? How great must the danger be? Or if we speak of *imminent* danger or *probable* danger, who is to judge them and by what criteria? These questions cannot be answered without the operation of common sense in the specific problematic situations out of which they arise.

When we speak of the "wisdom of the law," from the time of Solomon to our own, it is because it expresses these common-sense presuppositions, however overlaid with legalisms. When the law disregards them, we speak of the law as an ass —and rightly so.

Even though Holmes's doctrine does not by itself decide the specific cases which fall under it, we can see at once that it *includes* types—illustrated by the stock illustration of the man who falsely shouts "Fire!" in a crowded theater[38]—and that it *excludes* types of cases illustrated by those who, whether out of well-intentioned ignorance or not, advocate policies which are fraught with disaster. Most cases fall between these limiting types, but cluster around the first.

I shall not concern myself here with the history of the "clear and present danger" doctrine. It has now become a whole family of doctrines. A great legal scholar and civil libertarian who is not a ritualistic liberal believes it has been reduced to a phrase.[39] But even phrases are meaningful. Every variation in the doctrine from first to last is incompatible with the notion of absolute rights. This appears as explicitly as one can wish in Justice Brandeis's formulation:

But although the rights of free speech and assembly are fundamental, they are not in their nature absolute. Their exercise is

34

subject to their restriction, if the particular restriction proposed is required in order to protect the state from destruction or from serious injury, political, economic or moral . . . the necessity which is essential to a valid restriction does not exist unless speech would produce, or is intended to produce, a clear and imminent danger of some substantive evil which the state constitutionally may seek to prevent.[40]

When the doctrine is interpreted this way, clear lines of continuity can be drawn between this expression of realistic civil libertarianism and the distinctions recognized by Jefferson and Madison, who were far in advance of their time— an eloquent, valiant, but miniscular minority among their contemporaries. Jefferson's differentiation between "principle" and "rights of conscience," for which we are answerable only to God, and "overt acts against peace and order," for which we are answerable to civil government—although it does not explicitly concern itself with the marginal situations in which words are direct incitements to action—is the starting point for Holmes's and Brandeis's doctrine. The doctrine itself has been formulated in various ways and refined to take note of difficult borderline cases. No matter how it is formulated, its application depends upon the proper assessment of the facts. That is why it is possible to accept the doctrine and deny that it was legitimately applied by Holmes in the *Schenck* case. The danger at the time was neither clear nor present. Similarly, it is possible to accept the principles enunciated in Justice Frankfurter's remarkable opinions in the flag-saluting cases[41]—affirming the position that religious *practices* must fall within the jurisdiction of legislative competence—and disagree, as he did, with the wisdom of the state legislatures.

The stone of stumbling in many discussions of the doctrine is the overlapping in penumbral associations of the meanings of the expressions "advocacy" and "incitement." The terms are morally and legally neutral in meaning until we know what is being advocated or incited. Strictly speaking, whatever the moral quality of any particular expression of advocacy may be, legally there can be nothing objectionable in advocating, say, a policy of euthanasia, even if this runs counter to the feelings of the community. However, to incite an individual or group to practice euthanasia upon a helpless individual under existing laws would be legally wrong even if it did not run counter to the feelings of the community. The advocacy of euthanasia as a policy is legally unobjectionable because it presupposes that the proposal is to be submitted to the arbitrament of the democratic process.

Suppose, however, that in a democratic society one advocates the destruction of the democratic process—not as something to be decided through normal constitutional procedures, which is theoretically conceivable—but as something to be achieved by force and violence. As a mere proposal, considered *abstractly,* such a position would be comparable, to use a macabre illustration, to advocating cannibalism or murder as a fine art. Everyone can see the difference between such advocacy in general and inciting a particular murder. Why cannot people see the difference so clearly in *concrete* situations? The main reason is that in concrete situations the distinction is not so clear, and there is no substitute for knowledge and intelligence in resolving the questions of fact on which the distinction depends.

Scientific psychology, as well as contemporary philosophy of mind, reinforces the conclusion that whatever legal distinctions we make between "advocacy" and "incitement," in practice the distinction is functional. Traditional dualisms which isolate and insulate a man's ideas from the situational context in which they function, make ideas vapors of a ghost that inhabits but cannot activate the human machine. But analysis will show that once we distinguish between revery and belief, ideas are implicit plans of action, and that the way we determine whether we are entertaining two different ideas, or only one of them in different dress, is by their uses and consequences in behavior. Words trigger actions when they function as signals in situations in which human emotions have been keyed to the point of ready discharge. They play the same if a slightly delayed function when they are integral elements in the patterns of guided behavior. That is why and how ideas count in a material world. When they count in specific historical situations in such fashion as to incite, threaten, or create violence, they have no constitutional protection. One can tell whether they do this, not by examining the words or speech alone, but by examining them in the context of the embracing situation. The cold record of the utterance alone is hard to decipher. The language need not be hortatory. Not only the emotive but the practical and cognitive import of a judgment may be conveyed by declarative, interrogative, or, shall we say, imprecative sentence forms indifferently. Tone, pitch, gesture, and stance are relevant. In some situations it *may* be enough for a rabble rouser to say: "Lynching is too good for these rapists," or to ask: "Can Christians tolerate those who are guilty of ritual blood murders?" or to hypothecate: "If these strike breakers had broken legs, they would be unable to cross our picket lines," to put him outside the pale of constitutional tolerance *before* the lynching, pogrom, or bone breaking starts. Nor do words have to be heard. They may be read. There is a difference between a newspaper editorial which argues that some assassinations in history have had a beneficent effect and one which asserts that the assassination of a particular member of the community here and now would have such an effect.

In every case it is understood that the incitement which loses its right to expression is an incitement to an *illegal* action. We are not discussing incitements to attend an athletic rally or to turn aside the temptations of Satan. That is why so many people are bewildered when they hear jurists seriously maintain that the First Amendment throws its mantle of protection around verbal behavior which incites to actions that are clearly illegal. It explains the uneasiness with which, even in rather doctrinaire circles, Justice Black's pronouncement in *Yates* vs. *United States* was received. With the concurrence of Justice Douglas, he declared: "I believe that the First Amendment forbids Congress to punish people for talking about public affairs, whether or not such discussion *incites to action, legal or illegal.*" [42] On this reading, must the lynching or pogrom or riot actually begin before the goddess of liberty frowns and gives the command to intervene and punish? Although some of Justice Black's opinions have on occasion fallen short of consecutiveness of thought,[43] I hesitate to take his words on their face, since they flout the common-sense presuppositions of ordered society.

Presumably the operating phrase in the sentence quoted above is "public affairs." For I cannot conceive that any man, no less a distinguished jurist, would argue that one is, or should be, protected in talking about "private affairs" whether or not such talk "incites to action legal or illegal." The law protects me against the man who falsely accuses me of murder or even of giving short weight. And it does so even if I cannot show that any particular person's behavior toward me was altered or that my business was adversely affected in consequence. And were I to attempt to make such a showing in order to support a claim to punitive damage, would we not regard it as absurd for a defendant to say: "I did indeed express the opinion that he is a murderer and a thief. I even urged individuals to engage in certain actions towards him and refrain from others. But theirs is the responsibility for whatever action was taken, not mine. Since my opinions did not erupt into specific overt acts on my own part, I invoke the sanctuary of the sacred absolutes of the First Amendment."

But if talk about "public affairs" leads to consequences as bad as, or much worse than, this kind of talk about "private affairs," why should it enjoy constitutional protection? The reply may be that the democratic process cannot function unless the incitements to, and occurrences of, illegal action are accepted as its necessary price. But this is so far from being so that the opposite is more nearly true. The democratic process breaks down when the consequences of talk are violent or illegal actions.

There remains then the only other defense of this remarkable sentence. It may be argued that talk about "public affairs" can *never* incite to the kind of action which is prejudicial to the elementary necessities of civilized life. If this actually be so—and is not made so by definition—then there is no point in justifying talk about public affairs whether it "incites to action, legal or illegal." But it emphatically is not so! How shall we treat Communists is certainly a question about public affairs. If the treatment being proposed is an incitement to hang them, then in certain situations, not hard to imagine by anyone who lived through the period immediately after the First World War, such talk could transform a crowd into a lynching bee. Casper's proposals to solve the Negro problem and Rockwell's proposals to solve the Jewish problem are undoubtedly directed to public affairs. When propounded with demagogic skill before an ugly crowd in communities where tensions are running high, they may trigger off riot and even murder. They, like Communists, have a right to be protected in the advocacy of their doctrines, even against those who would forcibly prevent them from speaking and writing.[44] But at the point where their advocacy turns to incitement of violence, they lose their right to constitutional protection and may be legally punishable for the effects of their speech.

III

Despite the absolutist's interpretation of the Bill of Rights, situations keep arising in which the natural pragmatism of the normal mind revolts against the confining dogmas of what is everlastingly so. Common sense trickles out of the cracks and seams of the structure of rationalization as principles become strained. The result is sometimes very curious. Impassioned declaration of allegiance to the absolutist conception of some provisions of the Bill of Rights is coupled with a bewildering and dangerous relativistic interpretation of other provisions of the Bill of Rights.

Consider, for example, the position of a writer whose views have not been without influence—Dr. Alexander Meiklejohn. He proudly avows his absolutism but admits that "in any well-governed society, the legislature has the right and duty to prohibit certain forms of speech." [45] Indeed, the sentence is introduced with the phrase, "no one can doubt it." At the same time he insists that the First Amendment absolutely and unqualifiedly prohibits abridgment of speech. We are told in italics: (1) that the First Amendment *"does not forbid the abridging of speech,"* and (2) that it does forbid "the abridging of the freedom of speech." The paradox is allegedly resolved by the claim that the Bill of Rights provides for two kinds of freedom of speech—private and public. Private freedom of speech, which our common sense tells us is not absolutely privileged, is governed by the Fifth Amendment, according to which no one can be deprived of freedom—including, on this interpretation, freedom of speech—except by *due process* of law. Public freedom we can never be deprived of. It is absolute.

This contention that the Bill of Rights embodies two fundamentally different concepts of freedom, expressed in two different amendments, would be a momentous discovery, if true. So far as I know, no one has made this claim before. Of some significance is the fact that there is not a shred of historical evidence that this distinction was recognized by the Framers, and considerable evidence that it was not. The term "liberty" in the Fifth Amendment, as the context indicates, refers to imprisonment and not freedom of speech, whereas the phrase "freedom of speech" in the First Amendment covers an entire gamut of utterances and publications which by the widest stretch of the imagination could not reasonably be classified as public affairs.

The First Amendment protects me in my right, among other things, to express my belief or disbelief in immortality or in the hypothesis that the Earl of Oxford is the author of the plays attributed to Shakespeare, and in my right to publish free verse and paint abstractions. But what have these to do with public affairs—in the ordinary sense of the phrase?

The reading, therefore, that we are confronted with two entirely different kinds of speech—one to which we have an absolute right, and one to which we have not—must be treated not as a discovery but as a proposal. As a proposal it suffers from fatal difficulties. Either it begs all the questions at issue by *defining* speech about public affairs in such a way that it never conflicts with, or threatens, other constitutional rights like justice and public safety; or, if it does not so define it, it furnishes no guide whatsoever in the difficult task of determining when speech is about public affairs and when about private affairs. For in the ordinary sense of these words, there are many occasions—and these create the problems— in which speech about the one cannot be separated from speech about the other.

That Meiklejohn is really settling difficult problems by fiat or definition is apparent in his reading of the First Amendment as "saying that, as interests, the integrity of public discussion and the care for the public safety are identical." [46] But, of course, *if* they are identical! But whether they are or not identical depends upon the observation of consequences, not upon decree. Most of the time they are identical. Sometimes they definitely are not. If a public discussion seems about to culminate in a violent march against some unpopular minority, and there is every reason to believe that the only way to prevent the outbreak of violence is to stop the discussion, Meiklejohn would have to say that there was no genuine public discussion going on. And presumably, since the care for public safety is *identical* with the integrity of public discussion, he would have to say, where there is no question about the devotion to the public safety, no matter how exhibited, that it was *ipso facto* proof of devotion to the integrity of public discussion. This would be sheer intellectual violence to the decencies of proper usage.

On the view we are criticizing, the right to debate conscription is absolute; the right to counsel against conscription or to urge desertion is not. The right to discuss the wisdom of a policy of peace or war is absolute; when and where and how to discuss it is not. The second right may be regulated and abridged. Even during war the government must permit absolute freedom to discuss and advocate surrender to the enemy, but of course it has a right to lay down the ground rules prescribing when, where, and how. The right of citizens to assembly and petition is also absolute; but they can be told when, where, and how to assemble and petition. The distinction between two kinds of freedom of speech, combined with the high *apriorism* which disdains the assessment of empirical consequences in difficult and dangerous situations, actually generates a series of Pickwickian absolutes. One who really believes in absolute rights can very well say: "Thank you for nothing. What you gave me under the First Amendment, you make impossible for me to exercise under the Fifth. When I claim an absolute right to speak, I mean a right to speak regardless of the consequences of my speech on either the private or the public safety. And as I understand the English language, it is one thing to ascertain whether I am discussing public affairs and quite another whether I am concerned for the public safety." When anarchists or others damn concern for the public safety, shall we deny that they are discussing public affairs?

It is perfectly possible to say that the belief in freedom of speech is warranted by experience, that historically we have incontestable evidence that it enriches the quality of personal and public life and makes the community as a whole more secure rather than less so. And in places Dr. Meiklejohn does say this. However, he couples the assertion with the exaggerated and needless contention that because we believe that in the long run free speech does not endanger the security of the community, therefore we are never justified, even in a situation where it indisputably does endanger the security of the community, to abridge it. Certain things are true in the long run only because we use our intelligence to prevent disaster in the short run, which, if not forestalled, might well bring the run to a close. He himself admits that freedom of scientific research, which everyone will agree is beneficial to mankind, may under certain circumstances have to be abridged in certain fields of inquiry. There is no awareness of the analogous logic in cases in which the preservation of the freedoms of the people may require an abridgment of freedom of speech in an emergency.

It is the sober conviction that, in a society pledged to self-government, it is *never* true that, in the long run, the security of the nation is endangered by the freedom of the people. Whatever may be the immediate gains and losses, the dangers to our safety are *always* greater than the dangers to that society arising from political freedom. Suppression is *always* foolish. Freedom is *always* wise.[47]

I submit that experience has not established and cannot establish these propositions. Even if based on sober summaries of the past, which they are not, they would still be nothing more than declarations of hope for the future.

I submit that their plain implication that a self-governing society cannot function properly unless freedom of speech in political affairs is construed as an unabridgable absolute, is historically false, as a glance at other self-governing democratic communities of the twentieth century will show.

Troublesome questions arise when speech directed at persons clearly has political implications and when, in the course of public discussion, language is employed which violates a private interest. To call a public figure cowardly and incompetent may hurt his feelings, be unfair and even untrue. Yet the courts will not grant him redress because of our public interest in keeping discussion open, even when hard and uncharitable words are spoken. On the other hand, if a newspaper agitated by a great public issue charges falsely that an official has taken a bribe—or what is worse—that he is a secret member of the Communist party, the courts will find this actionable, and no plea that these charges were made in the course of a discussion of public affairs will be accepted in mitigation. It would be small consolation to those punished to be told that the penalties are being visited upon them under the Fifth—not the First—Amendment when in their own minds they are clearly engaging in a discussion of public affairs. One may even argue that when any man is slandered or libeled, every man's public interest is affected, since "the poisoning of the springs" of communication may be fatal to the health of a free society.

[handwritten margin note: but, / See / Pauling / v / Buckley]

The primary motivation of the Holmesian doctrine of the "clear and present danger" was to call attention to the long-run justification of the freedoms enumerated in the Bill of Rights in order to *enlarge* the provenance of their protection where hasty assessment was being made of their undesirable short-time effects in emergency situations or when passions were rife. It has by and large extended, not contracted, the areas of free communication in all domains by providing a principled formulation for intelligently grappling with the problems which arise in emergencies. Meiklejohn—and not he alone—has attacked in strongest terms Justice Holmes who fashioned, and others who have upheld and applied, this doctrine, as fundamentally confused minds. He charges that they have unwittingly sapped the foundations of American freedom.[48] It may be instructive, therefore, to examine the implications of his own position for freedom of expression in its broadest sense.

Freedom of speech and press are for him not merely or even primarily freedom from interference. Freedom must be a freedom *for* something, a freedom for self-governing men to educate themselves properly so that through the processes of communication they may achieve knowledge of the true and the good. "What, we must ask, would be the use of giving American citizens freedom to speak if they had nothing worth saying to say?" [49] Only educated men can be free. And whatever interferes with proper education is not really an exercise of the freedom of mind which the First Amendment was designed to protect. Speech which uses the radio, television, motion picture, newspapers, and other forms of publication for "the enslavement of our minds and wills" cannot properly be called free and consequently cannot be privileged under the First Amendment.

The radio as it now operates among us is not free. Nor is it entitled to the protection of the First Amendment. It is not engaged in the task of enlarging and enriching human communication. It is engaged in making money. . . .

The radio as we now have it, is not cultivating those qualities of taste, of reasoned judgment, of integrity, of loyalty, of mutual understanding upon which the enterprise of self-government depends. On the contrary, it is a mighty force for breaking them down. It corrupts both our morals and our intelligence.[50]

What Dr. Meiklejohn says of the radio can be said, and has been often said, of the press too.

Presumably, since the protection of the First Amendment would be lifted from such expressions of freedom, there could be no principled objection to legislation to control the mode, the style, and even the level of content of our communications industry—including the press—to see that they reach a sufficiently high cultural plane. This could easily open the door to censorship in the interest of political virtue. It could do more. It could invite government control of the press. Not only is private speech, as Meiklejohn understands it, palpably endangered by his refusal to include it in the scope of the First Amendment; even public speech could easily be curbed by indirection and subterfuge, by imposing on newspapers and other avenues of communication procedures to prevent the corruption of "both our morals and our intelligence." In effect, we would have truth-in-opinion acts operating under the guise of procedural rules. All this is hard to justify on the basis of the philosophy of democratic self-government, and reinforces the weight of the severe criticism made by Ernest Nagel and other critics of the totalitarian potential in Meiklejohn's educational and political philosophy.[51] The Republic of Plato is not the Republic of Thomas Jefferson or of Oliver Wendell Holmes. The general will of Rousseau—that compound of vicious mysticism and verbal legerdemain—had no influence on the thought of the authors of the First Amendment. Where communication is free, there will always be a danger that morals and intelligence will be corrupted. No attempt to prevent or eliminate such danger can be realistically conceived without some governmental control, and usually by the worst forms of such control—namely, by prior licensing or censorship which is subject to corruptions far worse than those it seeks to ward off.

The faith of a democrat is that political wisdom and virtue will sustain themselves in the free market of ideas without government controls so long as the channels of communication are kept open. What Jefferson said of religious doctrine is true of all doctrine so long as it is doctrine. "It is error alone which needs the support of government. Truth can stand alone." If this faith cannot be sustained by experience, democracy cannot endure as a viable government for fallible man.

IV

The view that human rights of any kind depend to some extent for their validity upon their consequences on the public good or public welfare is not without its difficulties. And this irrespective of whether the public good or welfare is defined substantively as a complex of interrelated rights or procedurally in terms of the processes of rational discussion by which conflicting rights are negotiated. Many critics of utilitarianism have explored the consequences of the view that any claim to a right must be appraised in relation to the public welfare or its effects upon others. Their conclusions have been mainly variations on the theme that, in the words of A. C. Ewing, "This is an admission which it is difficult to avoid and yet dangerous to make." [52] It is difficult to avoid for reasons already given. It is dangerous to make because it can be so readily abused. The very concept of public good or welfare, or even of public order and safety, is ambiguous— although not more so than the concept of liberty or freedom. Many tyrannical actions have been justified by reference to it. Some absolutists have contended that once a basic right is abridged, then in principle the difference between a free and open society and a totalitarian society disappears. Think of the crimes which have been committed in the name of law and order! This sometimes invites the retort: they usually follow the crimes committed in the name of liberty! Think of them! Such exchanges of admonitory warnings and epithets are unprofitable if they estop further reflection. By all means let us think of and avoid both kinds of excesses. Let us grant in addition the fallibility of all mortals, the presence of the tyrant in the rebel, and every tyrant's exacerbated sensibility to tyrannies greater than his own. Nonetheless, I do not believe that the admitted danger of abuse justifies the equation in principle drawn by absolutists between the necessary limitation of some rights in situations of conflict and the loss of rights in a closed society.

The reasons are many. Before presenting them I wish to advert briefly to a mode of argument in social and political affairs which may be called the argument of the "slippery slope." This mode of thinking takes its point of departure from the fact that conflict of principles or values sometimes compels us to take a necessary risk whose dangers are manifest. It then asks: where does one stop? And since in advance no one can indicate a specific stopping point, it assumes that one can never stop but that once we step on the slippery slope we must descend at an accelerated speed into the dread abyss of catastrophe, however conceived. There have been individuals who have protested against the introduction of fluorides, which are a poison, into drinking water as a preventive of caries on the ground that once we begin to add poisons, who knows where we will stop. We may end up by adding cyanide. Of course there are better arguments against fluoridation of drinking water than this, but, fanciful as it is, the argument has been employed. One will on occasion read that if a law approving of euthanasia under careful, controlled, medical and legal conditions were adopted, this would begin a slide toward genocide. The commonest argument against any abridgment of any specific, desirable freedom is that once we begin, we will end in the complete abridgment of all our other desirable freedoms. These shrill and false Cassandra cries have rent the air for decades.[53] The risks and losses of abridgment, to be sure, are always there. So are the risks and losses of refusing to make the abridgment in moments of great emergency. The abridgment is an incipient tendency which, if unchecked, *may* result in our hurtling down the slope. Every specific act contains the germ of a habit. But our very *aware-*

47

ness that we have stepped on a slope is a brake on our precipitous descent. Once we venture, as we sometimes must, on a dangerous course which may lead to our salvation in a particular situation but which may also be the beginning of our path to perdition, the only answer we can give to the question: "Where will you stop?" is *"Wherever our intelligence tells us to stop!"* Our intelligence may tell us not to begin—but if so, it must indicate a better way of solving the problematic difficulty created by the conflict of a duality or multiplicity of values.

A great need or national emergency arises. Congress decides that in meeting this need some right or freedom may have to be suspended in order to preserve the rest of our freedoms— perhaps the freedom to visit certain countries which have declared their hostility in cold war or hot. Now this sacrifice of freedom is to be deplored. It is bad in itself. But its exercise, in the particular circumstances, may be even worse. The sacrifice *may* lead to the sacrifice of other freedoms, to a toboggan down the slippery slope. But this sentence also means: it may *not*. Whether we can reasonably assert that it probably will or not, depends upon our knowledge and our willingness to make further inquiry. Justice Black is correct when he writes: "If the need is great, the right of government *can always be said* to outweigh the rights of the individual." [54] What he unfortunately ignores is that it is not a matter of *saying* but whether what is said is *true* or *false*. And we cannot find out by intoning pieties as we burke the challenge of finding out.

In the process of finding out what to do when the national need or emergency is great, it is false to imply that another national need—the national need to preserve the structure of our existing freedoms—is necessarily disregarded. When the decision is intelligent, this need actually controls in the sense that the health of the organism as a whole controls a medical decision on how to treat an affected part. Sometimes it is necessary to starve the stomach for the sake of the heart. This may be an unwise decision, but hardly on the ground that there is a grave risk that what begins with a prescription of austerity may end in a sentence of starvation.

In the process of finding out, we may discover that it is just as false to counterpose the right of government to the rights of the individual. The issue may be the question whether the rights of some individuals should outweigh in this particular situation the rights of other individuals from the point of view of the rights of all individuals. The presuppositions are that we are committed to the protection of all rights of all individuals and that it has been established in the situation at hand that they cannot all be fulfilled.

To be sure, when we solve a problem we are committing ourselves to more than just this problem, especially in law and morals. Nonetheless the life of mind is a succession of problems which cannot all be settled at once. This makes the readiness for reflection before new problems, rather than the regurgitation of absolutes, the decisive consideration.

Let us concretize the analysis by examining an illustration of the uncritical "argument from the slippery slope" and observe where it leads us.

Congress, on the advice of responsible officials and on the basis of evidence presented, passes a law, approved by the President, that any citizen who voluntarily votes in foreign political elections will be deemed to have expatriated himself or to have forfeited his citizenship. It is obvious that the conduct of our foreign relations, which falls within the powers of the Congress and Executive and not of the Supreme Court, could be very seriously embarrassed and, in certain situations, jeopardized by such action. In close elections abroad, dangerous political capital can be made out of these actions by American citizens.

One can raise the question whether reasonable grounds exist for believing that such actions *in fact* have these undesirable consequences. This is a matter of informed opinion and expertise, on which the judiciary is unlikely to be as qualified as those constitutionally entrusted with foreign affairs. One can challenge the action of Congress by asserting that native citizenship, or citizenship once properly acquired,

49

is "inalienable" and can be renounced only by the citizen himself. But if it is acknowledged that Congress has the authority and power to determine what voluntary actions of a citizen abroad can be construed as indicating such renunciation, the meaning of "inalienable" becomes Pickwickian if not downright bizarre. Finally, one can raise the question whether a particular vote of a particular citizen abroad is reasonably classifiable as participation in a foreign political election. Without contesting the general principle, a citizen may petition for redress on the ground that his action does not fall under it. A court that intelligently interprets the law may rule that a vote of an American summer visitor in a Swiss village on whether to hold a carnival this month or next does not constitute participation in a foreign political election as Congress understood it. Courts have engaged in much more difficult and strained feats of interpretation than is required by this obvious common-sense distinction.

Questions of the above sort are intelligible and relevant no matter how answered. But what shall we say of a position which argues in effect that if voting in a foreign election is considered sufficient ground for declaring American citizenship forfeit, then this may very well lead to regarding the following actions as also grounds warranting expatriation: criticizing the Secretary of State or an act of Congress or the President in the field of foreign affairs, advocating diplomatic recognition of Red China, disapproving the Eisenhower doctrine, accepting an invitation to speak as a private American citizen over the British radio, as George Kennan did in delivering the Reith Lectures? We slide to the very bottom of the slippery slope with the question: "If casting a ballot abroad is sufficient to deprive an American of his citizenship, why could not like penalties be imposed on the citizen who expresses disagreement with the nation's foreign policy in any of the ways enumerated?" [55]

This question, actually asked by Justices Douglas and Black, has a simple answer. Voting in a foreign election is a reasonable sign that the individual considers himself to be a member of another national community. If tolerated by the United States, the country of his original nationality, it could be interpreted by other nations as direct intervention in *their* domestic affairs. It therefore embarrasses the conduct of our foreign affairs in a way that the litany of possible criticisms of the foreign policy of our own country does not even remotely approximate. Further, there is not the slightest positive contribution to our own democratic processes in voting abroad—an action which if done en masse may lead to rupture of relations between nations and perhaps worse. On the other hand, all the types of criticism directed by our citizens at our foreign policy are integral to our whole concept of the democratic process. They are precious to us, the people of the United States, no matter how embarrassing to our officials. The right of an American citizen to vote in a foreign election by no fantasy of imagination can be conceived as embodied in the American Bill of Rights; but there would be no Bill of Rights if criticism of our officials were penalized by loss of citizenship.

To assume, therefore, that from the reasonable decision to regard voting in foreign elections as a forfeiture of citizenship there is a strong likelihood that, by a succession of related steps, we shall end up by depriving a person of his citizenship, if he voices any criticism of the government's foreign policy, is so farfetched as to border on the absurd. There is a wide abyss which separates one from the other. It would be time enough to step in and cry havoc if the first small step were taken toward the abyss. In this instance, as in some others, the argument from the slippery slope rests not on judicious analysis but on wild prediction.

V

Why is it false to say that there is no difference in principle between the civil libertarian who rejects absolutism and the totalitarian who pleads the public welfare or common good as a pretext for his terroristic rule? The first reason is apparent as soon as we distinguish between the government or administration (or the state narrowly conceived), on the one hand, and the society or community, on the other. The public interest is not the interest of any set of rulers or administrators but obviously relates to the welfare of the community. Since the interests of the individuals and groups which make up the community conflict, the public interest or good must emerge from a process of reasonable weighing, of adjustment or reconciliation in a process where *all* interests must have public voice and representation. The public interest cannot therefore be fairly established when imposed arbitrarily from above by a governing regime not responsible to control by the democratic process. Consequently, when a right is abridged in a democratic community, the character of the action, even if we consider it mistaken, is *toto caelo* different, when due process has been observed, from a decree of a totalitarian regime which defines the public interest as it sees fit. Is there no difference except one of mere degree among the processes of exploration, persuasion, and debate by which consensus is established in free societies to make exception to their own rules and the arbitrary repressions of police states? If this is considered merely a matter of degree, it is true only in the sense in which differences in degree make an immediate difference between life and death. It is certainly true that Fascist, Communist, and totalitarian governments defend their infamies on the ground that they serve the public welfare or the common good. But what makes them totalitarian is precisely that they never give those who are ruled the right to govern themselves, and therewith the right to determine what the public or the common good is and what serves it best.

This distinction between the processes of decision in closed and open societies goes to the essence of the matter. It should be brought to bear on almost every general principle which presumably holds for both types of societies, so that their differences, wherever relevant, appear. Thus, one might agree with Hobbes that all rulers try to derive their duties and justify their actions by the maxim "The safety of the people is the supreme law." But the political meaning of this maxim has an entirely different significance depending upon

who the rulers are—a despot or a representative assembly—
how the safety of the people is determined and by whom.
Not to mention, of course, what is included under the phrase
"safety of the people," and the fact that in an open society
Hobbes's maxim may be disputed on moral grounds. Considerations of justice may override considerations of safety.

Second, no community, even of anarchists, can escape the
necessity of choice when allegedly absolute rights conflict—
and in grave situations, as we have seen, they always conflict. If blind impulse or brute force is not to resolve the conflict, reflective balancing of the interests and claims at stake
must resolve it as best it can. I am aware that reference to
the "balancing approach," where the freedoms of the Bill of
Rights are concerned, is anathema to absolutists. But every
judicial opinion ever written which upholds one liberty
over against another, or against any other social claim or
expressly granted power of Congress, adopts a balancing
approach irrespective of the language employed. When he
must acknowledge this fact, the absolutist shifts his grounds.
He now asserts that he never intended to deny the necessity
of balancing conflicting interests or conflicting liberties, for
these are indeed unavoidable. He contends, however,

that the Framers themselves did this balancing when they wrote
the Constitution and the Bill of Rights. They appreciated the
risks involved and they decided that certain rights should be
guaranteed regardless of these risks. Courts [and *a fortiori*, Con-
gress] have neither the right nor the power to review this original
decision of the Framers and to make a different evaluation of the
importance of the rights granted in the Constitution. Where conflicting values exist in the field of individual liberties protected
by the Constitution, that document settles the conflict . . . [56]

Does it? What does the Constitution tell us to do in the
event that the fair trial requirements of the Fifth and Sixth
amendments conflict with the free speech protection of the
First—a not infrequent occurrence? When does free speech
about a trial make an individual liable to contempt of court,
when not? It is not the Constitution which tells the judge

when speech or publication constitutes contempt of court but the circumstances of the case read in the light of an informed intelligence. Sometimes the judge sacrifices the rights of a defendant—to a degree quite shocking to the moral sensibilities of our British cousins—because of the importance of the public's right to know. Sometimes he fines or jails the enterprising reporter and publisher despite their shrill cries about freedom of speech.

The passage quoted above continues with the observation "and its policy should not be changed without constitutional amendments by the people in the manner provided by the people." But which policy is here in question? The Constitution does *not* formulate a policy on the conflicting values in the field of individual liberties. It tells us to treasure freedom of speech *and* the right to a fair trial. It does not tell us which one gets priority when they conflict. It expresses the values which are to serve as guides in applying general rules and prohibitions. It no more formulates specific policies of priority when these values, rules, and prohibitions conflict than it defines terms like "unreasonable searches and seizures," "due process of law," "cruel and unusual punishment," "just compensation"—all of which appear in the Bill of Rights. The Constitution, no matter how often amended, is not a recipe book or manual on how to mix or balance ingredient rights. Jefferson may have been a poor prophet about many things, as when he wrote: "The true barriers of our liberty in this country are our State governments." [57] But to those overwhelmed with piety for the original wisdom with which the Framers balanced conflicts of interests and values, his well-known words about men who "look at Constitutions with sanctimonious reverence, and deem them like the ark of the covenant, too sacred to be touched" [58] are still worth pondering.

Third, it is a profound error to conceive of balancing as if it were a process of value deliberation in which all elements have *equal* weight, as if nothing had been historically and politically established by its fruits in experience, and every decision taken with the innocence and freshness of the first morning of man. There are presumptions of validity which, even if not final, are still presumptions, which give overwhelming weight to freedom of press when this interferes with freedom from litter of city streets, or to freedom of expression when this disturbs another person's peace of mind.

How is it with ordinary moral reasoning? Can any moral imperatives be more categorical than those which enjoin us against lying, stealing, or abandoning the helpless? When we balance other interests—even other moral interests—against them, do we start from scratch and with nice impartiality equate all competing interests? This would be to exhibit moral cretinism, a sign that a thinking machine had run amok. These imperatives have a tremendous moral authority because of their experienced quality and because of the cumulative evidence of their worth in establishing the faith and trust on which civilized society rests. Nonetheless, a categorical imperative against concealing or denying the truth in some extreme situations may conflict with our duty to our country, with our sense of compassion or mercy, with our sense of honor and filial devotion. One need not invent these moral dilemmas and tragic situations. Existentialism did not discover the agonies of choice in extreme situations. History is replete with them. They are part of the human estate. In balancing principle against principle, imperative against imperative, interest against interest, it is false to say that we condemn the value which ultimately must be overridden when the balance is struck. On the contrary, it is because we treasure what must be sacrificed that the choice is often poignant, and sometimes tragic.

The logic of choice is fundamentally the same with respect to the freedoms of the Bill of Rights, and is manifestly different from the decisions made by those who hold power in totalitarian states. The totalitarian decisions flow from "reasons of state," which may be merely interests of party and sometimes no more than reasons of a maniacal ego. These reasons of state or interests *automatically* take precedence over all other conflicting rights and decencies. Democratic decisions, on the other hand, give priority to the freedoms of the Bill of Rights, first because of their moral quality, second because of their historical justification, and third because of their *strategic role* in the preservation of the whole structure of freedom which constitutes self-government and the democratic way of life. These are the reasons why the freedoms of the Bill of Rights and certain other constitutional provisions have a prima facie validity over all other apparently justified claims in situations of conflict—a validity or priority which is not constitutional but historical, determined not by their place in the text but by our intelligent reading of our past in the light of our desirable goals in the present. These are the reasons why we cheerfully put up with their costs in irritation, inefficiency, and delay, and why we are very reluctant to abridge them even if such abridgment proves inescapable. When we give a right a preferred position in a situation in which it conflicts with another, it is *not,* as Justice Douglas puts it, "because it is a grant absolute in terms" [59] of a text but because of its key position in the life of a self-governing community. This is what it means for these rights to have prima facie validity. But prima facie validity is not absolute validity, a strategic role is not an absolute role.

Justice Learned Hand has been severely criticized by absolutists because he observed that the freedoms enumerated in the Bill of Rights and the Constitution are "admonitions" to Congress of what to avoid. The word "admonition" is unfortunate because it suggests the pale warning of a schoolmaster or a fond ineffectual parent. I have tried to express with greater force and persuasiveness what I take to be Justice Hand's meaning. But whether called admonitions, moral imperatives of government, commands, they must function, in Jefferson's own words, as "general rules to which there may be proper exceptions." [60]

We must conclude, therefore, that the contention that denial of absolute civil liberties is tantamount to acceptance in principle of a police state has no more logic in it than the contention that because no man is morally perfect there is no difference in principle between the conscientiously up-right man and the wantonly criminal one.

VI

My emphasis upon the *strategic* importance of the Bill of Rights is designed in part to challenge the false antithesis drawn between the individual and the social in many defenses of inherent personal rights. It is a commonplace of philosophical analysis that the individual and the social are not substantive entities but adjectival distinctions in a unitary cultural process. As bodies, human beings are particulars—they are not yet individuals or personalities. Nor can they become so except in a context of social relations. Social relations are internal relations as far as human personalities are concerned. This is not a dogma of John Dewey's allegedly social-all-too-social philosophy. Despite his different metaphysical bias, Whitehead, too, recognizes this. "The whole concept of absolute individuals with absolute rights, and with a contractual power of forming fully defined external relations has broken down. The human being is inseparable from its environment in each occasion of its existence. The [social] environment which the occasion inherits is immanent in it, and conversely it is immanent in the environment which it helps to transmit." [61] Whatever we have learned in psychology, sociology, social history, and cultural anthropology reinforces the evidence of the *interdependence* of men —and, in this age of modern science, technology, and economy, of their *growing* interdependence.

The justifications of the Bill of Rights in the past have been formulated as if their most cogent and persuasive grounds were that they furthered certain private and personal goods *against* the incursions of a state power conceived as something inherently hostile and foreign to individuals—as something standing separate, apart, and over the community of one's neighbors, as something designated by "them," "the others," "the enemy." But a much more effective justification of the freedoms of the Bill of Rights can be found in their beneficial social consequences. To those who would curb freedom in the interests of a securer and more prosperous society, we can point to the impressive record of how freedom has paid off socially, so to speak, in the beneficial consequences of keeping open the pathways of new inquiry, in the advantages of proposing and exploring all relevant alternatives—even hateful, distasteful, and mistaken ones. The conquest of nature and space, of plague and disease has kept pace with the extension of freedom of inquiry from field to field. To achieve successes in these areas, even totalitarian societies have been compelled to relax their ideological controls. It was only when they abandoned their ideological taboo against the theory of relativity in physics and the theory of resonance in chemistry that the Russian Communists made technical advances of importance. Where the blighting hand of dogma rested heavily, as in genetics, they marked time.

One of the commonest arguments for the toleration of error is the weakest of arguments. Suppression, we are told, is self-defeating, for in the end the doctrines or individuals persecuted are sure to thrive. But this is a wishful misreading of history which is full of successful suppressions.[62] To say that suppression is impossible is not only false, it sometimes provokes bigoted absolutists, who are convinced they possess the final truth, to show that what is declared impossible can with sufficient zeal be done. No, the much better argument for toleration is the social uses of error. Morris R. Cohen as well as Karl Popper have argued that the growth of science depends, at least in important part, upon tracing the consequences of false hypotheses. Similarly, growth in public enlightenment can result from the drawing and elaboration of the consequences of any social doctrine, no matter how heretical or extreme—provided that a proper climate of opinion encourages the development of the doctrine, and provided its espousal remains in the universe of discourse and debate. It is one thing to present reasoned argument for the abolition of the progressive income tax, or of any tax; it is quite another to incite others to refuse to pay their taxes.

Despite its simplism, the view that the government or state power is necessarily the enemy of politically free men in a self-governing society still casts a long and deep shadow on current discussions of individual rights. Granted that the occasions on which most rights were asserted in the past— and particularly in American colonial experience—were those in which the state power, wielded by a small class not responsible to those they governed, was clearly oppressive or threatened oppression. Granted that the influence of the American frontier contributed to strengthen and stereotype the view that the state was only a restraining institution with irritating police and tax powers. Granted further that in Europe, declarations of the rights of man were directed against states that were largely feudal in their legal and political structure. This is sufficient to justify distrust of state power. Out of this experience developed the insights which are among the permanent contributions of American political thought—the necessity of checking power by power, and perpetual vigilance against the abuse of delegated power.

There are two generic ways of preventing abuse of power. One is to see that it is not used, or that it is used as little as possible. The other, and much more difficult way, is to devise institutional safeguards against abuse while using it. Where the state is clearly the enemy—"they" who are no part of "us" —it is better to prevent it from using power. The less government, the better for the freedoms of all. But now the state responds to democratic controls in many ways with which historical developments in America and Western Europe have made us familiar. It is no longer merely an uneasy servant that bears watching lest it reach out for mastery. It must be encouraged to action against *other* potential enemies of freedom that have appeared on the scene and grown to giant size when the state was the chief object of national distrust— unregulated industry and business, economic monopoly which does its own regulation, sprawling and unhygienic urbanization, and other serious consequences of the industrial revolution. The state must exercise, not restrain, its power to prevent the pauperization and social degradation of its

Bah!

citizens—evils which if unchecked are likely to erode its free political institutions. The state must become more than the umpire of a political game whose integrity is inescapably suspect. It must regulate and control those social and economic processes which if unchecked tend to corrupt both players and umpire. The more the state reaches out to sustain the economic welfare and health of all its citizens, the less it can be reasonably viewed as *inherently* an enemy.

It was none other than Jefferson himself who realized, without explicitly admitting it, that the preservation of political rights by themselves is not sufficient to preserve the heritage of freedom. "Let our workshops remain in Europe," he pleaded, for he feared the effects of the industrial revolution on a free society. "The mobs of the great cities add just as much to the support of pure government as sores do to the strength of the human body." [63] And for the great European cities he knew at firsthand, this was undoubtedly true. There is a clear prescience in Jefferson that the social, economic, and cultural forces in society must in the end have an enormous, and potentially dangerous, impact upon the state of political freedom. What he did *not* see or say clearly is that the state must have a positive role in regulating and influencing these forces in the very interests of the very political freedoms which were dearest to him.

The same Constitution which enshrined the political rights of the American people, and which the economic royalists of *laissez faire* had interpreted as absolutes forbidding social welfare legislation, provided the documentary warrant, without the necessity of formal amendment, to win for the government powers to effect social and economic changes undreamed of in his day or, if dreamed of, seen as nightmares. "Were we directed from Washington when to sow and when to reap," wrote Jefferson, "we should soon want bread." Given the state of communications in his day, this would very probably have been true. Today when farmers are directed from Washington what to sow and when to reap, we suffer no want of bread. Thirty years ago when farmers sowed and reaped what and when they pleased, many of them

hah!

went without bread. It would be difficult to convince American workers that the government or state which gave them the legal rights to organize and bargain collectively—something many of them could not win for themselves by their own power—which gave them the multiple, even if still inadequate, protections of present-day social welfare—that this state was an enemy whose inherent tendency to get out of hand must be kept in automatic check. Eternal vigilance against the state—as against every other aggregation of power in society—must still be retained lest the state diminish men as it seeks to improve their lives. But eternal vigilance as a slogan, as a set of attitudes which views all government controls as manacles upon the mind and body—whether in education or medicine or business—is not the price of freedom but the guarantee of social stagnation and reaction.

Unfortunately, this view of government still widely prevails. Muted for some years during the era of the New Deal, which saved those who held this view from the consequences of its folly, it is now reasserting itself in louder and more confident tones. It crops up in surprising places. The dean of one of the nation's largest law schools has proclaimed that the root idea of the American Constitution is "that man can be free, that political processes can in truth be democratic only when, and only because, the state is not free." [64] A more misleading simplification would be hard to pen.

By way of summary, I can point to at least three crucial truths which this interpretation underplays, and sometimes overlooks. First, the paradoxical fact that a man can be free only because other men are not free to prevent him, and that, in consequence, unless the state is free to forestall this prevention and enforce a man's freedom, no man can be free. Second, the empirical fact that, in our world of modern science, technology, and industry, men can use their political freedom most effectively to further the values of an open society only when the state is also free to help create the social and economic conditions of a free culture. Third, the paradoxical fact that in the inescapable conflict of rights and duties, obligations and responsibilities, there can be no absolute obligation except—in John Erskine's memorable phrase —the moral obligation to be intelligent. Intelligence alone is an absolute value because, as distinct from love, kindness, knowledge, courage, freedom, and every other value which is a constituent of the good life, intelligence alone is the judge of its own limitations. It mediates the conflicts of all other values, and sets limits of scope, timing, and appropriateness to their expression. It possesses a quality of intrinsic delight in addition to its instrumental function. It knows when to be quiescent, when to take a holiday—when it can give rein to the vital impulses. But it never abdicates.

The real challenge to democratic government is whether the locus of the ultimate authority on which every government must rest can be found in the processes of intelligence as they develop from the matrix of freely given consent—or whether it must be entrusted to a special group of guardians, philosophical or judicial.

2

Democracy
and Judicial Review

ANY HAVE BEEN the meanings given to the
term "democracy" in the history of thought.
Rhetorical expressions of allegiance to democracy and passionate commitment to its defense
tell us little until we understand how the term "democracy" is to be interpreted. We know from contemporary
experience as well as the historical record the wide variety of
its connotations and their emotive associations. The very
term "democracy" was not in good repute among the influential opinion makers when the United States Constitution was
framed. Jefferson was one of the few who braved the suspi-
cions of his day. He both called himself and was widely regarded as a democrat. And what a democrat! On the morning
of Jefferson's inauguration, John Marshall wrote to his inti-
mate friend, Pinckney: "The Democrats are divided into
speculative theorists and absolute terrorists. With the latter
I am disposed to class Mr. Jefferson . . . If he ranges himself
with them, it is not difficult to foresee that much difficulty is
in store for our country; if he does not they will soon become
his enemies and calumniators." [1] By "terrorist," Marshall

could hardly have meant one who practiced terrorism of the deed. He was probably referring by this designation to a terrorism of reason whose fruits he saw in the French Revolution, of which Jefferson had approved while strongly deploring its excesses. And it is quite true that Jefferson did place supreme confidence in human reason, which always terrifies those who are fearful lest its exercise weaken the absolutes they hold most dear. "Fix reason firmly in her seat," he wrote, "and call to her tribunal every fact, every opinion. Question with boldness even the existence of God; because if there be one, he must approve of the homage of reason, than that of blindfolded fear." [2]

It was Jefferson too who in his letters and state papers helped fix the prevalent concept of the meaning of democracy, by indicating what the minimal conditions were in the absence of which the use of the term "democratic" strikes us today as arbitrary if not a semantic outrage. No democracy can exist which does not recognize the responsibility of governmental power to the adult citizens affected by its decisions. This responsibility requires the operating presence, not paper indication, of mechanisms of freely given consent and control. By virtue of their operation, the dominant trends of public opinion about general or specific questions of public welfare determine public policy.

However the public welfare is defined, in a democracy it is something which, when interests of groups conflict, must be established through the uncoerced processes of discussion, debate, and inquiry. The just powers of government rest upon the consent of the governed. But this proposition cannot be simply converted. Not everything which rests upon the consent of the governed is just. Democratic government is not necessarily good government even when it is responsible government. It is sometimes foolish, sometimes callous and hostile to the underprivileged. Nonetheless, the faith of the democrat, from Jefferson to Lincoln to Dewey, has rested on the belief that democratic government or self-government, provides the best, although far from perfect, way of getting good government. The fundamental challenge to this faith was formulated, not by Hitler or Stalin or other totalitarians who profess to be democrats of a sort in order to destroy democratic institutions more effectively, but by Plato and his philosophic descendants. They contend that most human beings are either too stupid or too vicious or both to be entrusted with the powers of self-government, and that ultimately the best interests of the people can be furthered by a government of the learned, the wise, and the virtuous. This hardy political perennial blooms in many different forms of argument, and is found in both conservative and liberal color.

The reply of the intelligent defender of the democratic faith to Plato and his latter-day followers is not to deny that democratic government is incapable of injustice, foolishness, and sometimes cruel and unnecessary oppression. He denies, first, that wisdom or virtue can be identified with technological knowledge or expertness. He denies further, even if wisdom and virtue are forms of knowledge, that any select group has a monopoly of them—or, to put it in another idiom, he denies that it is necessary to be an expert to appraise critically the work of experts. He believes that the acknowledged abuses of democratic rule can be countered by a multiplicity of educational activities aimed at the enlightenment of the citizenry. He points out that whatever the deficiencies of democratic rule, the historical record suggests that the deficiences of alternative systems are much worse. This strengthens the hope that the processes of political enlightenment will make democratic government and its representative bodies more sensible and responsible. Senators Claghorn and Bunkum and their similars on other legislative levels will be progressively retired.

One historic answer to this position is that it is unduly optimistic. There will always be demagogues in representative bodies, and by the time they are retired, if ever, they may inflict grievous wounds on the democratic body politic. The people themselves may become a mob, swept by passion and hate, or may become the mindless, consenting medium of politically ambitious leaders, manipulated by a sensationalist press. There are other means of preventing abuses of democratic power by the highest instances of the popular will. The best and historically well-tried means of doing so, it is said, is through judicial review by a body of non-elected judges who hold tenure for life.

The theme of judicial review is vastly complex. My primary concern in this chapter will be to determine whether the power of judicial review is compatible with the theory and logic of democracy; and whether, if not, its existence is nonetheless historically essential to make democratic life viable in the United States. It is necessary to distinguish between these two points. In the past it was commonly charged by liberal thinkers that judicial review of the highest legislative authority was inherently or intrinsically undemocratic. Conservatives rarely thought it necessary to deny this—it seemed patently so. In contradistinction to democratic critics of judicial review, they were firmly convinced that it was necessary to include an anti-democratic check on the functioning of our democratic political system in order to prevent "the dictatorship of the majority"—that bugaboo which haunts the books of political theorists but has never been found in the flesh in modern history. Only in our own period have we heard impassioned defenses of the democratic character of the process of judicial review itself. One recent and not uninfluential view maintains that no law can be properly regarded as the law of democratic American society until it has been validated by the United States Supreme Court.[3] Since the overwhelming majority of the laws in both state legislatures and Congress never come before the Supreme Court, and have therefore never been validated, their status in this view would be gravely problematic. The very extremity of this view is highly significant. It shows that the strange shifts in ideological perspective toward the Supreme Court—the reëvaluations of the character and justifications of judicial review in our generation—do not merely depend, as is sometimes alleged, upon *who* is doing the reviewing or upon whose ox is being gored in the process. This, even if to some extent true, is a nearsighted practical opportunism, which, because it is always present, may be ignored in the

66

quest for a principled clarity. No, this view which stresses the democratic role of the Supreme Court suggests rather that a new theoretical compound is being distilled from a fresh analysis of American history and the facts of political power.

Since by judicial review I shall refer only to the power of the United States Supreme Court to nullify *Congressional* legislation and Executive action, and not to its functions as a supreme court in the national system of law which of necessity entails the power to override *state* legislatures, it may be of interest to recall that no Supreme Court justice in the past has ever been so bold as to make the claim that the power of review over the highest organ of legislative and executive authority is itself democratic. On the contrary, even when it has been justified, it has often been done in ways which emphasized its undemocratic if not arbitrary character. "We are under a Constitution," observed Chief Justice Hughes, "but the Constitution is what the judges say it is." [4] And as everyone knows, the judges do not always say the same thing even about the same provisions; so we must amend this dictum to read that the Constitution is what a majority of justices say it is until they unsay it. This does not sound very democratic.

Concerning the power of the Court to read the Constitution and check the trespasses of Congress, Chief Justice Stone's biting reminder to his colleagues is pertinent. "While unconstitutional exercise of power by the executive and legislative branch of the government is subject to judicial restraint, the only check upon our own exercise of power is our own sense of self-restraint." [5] Until recently it is not likely that any fair-minded person, even if he approved of judicial review, would have disagreed with Justice Frankfurter's sober statement that "judicial review is a deliberate check upon democracy through an organ of government not subject to popular control." [6] Even the doctrine of judicial activism, to which influential members of the present Court subscribe, has been strongly challenged by some of their brethren. Justice Jackson maintained that this doctrine, which justifies constant and easy readiness to set aside Congressional enactments that appear unconstitutional, is "wholly incompatible with faith in democracy, and insofar as it encourages a belief that judges may be left to correct the result of public indifference to issues of liberty in choosing Presidents, Senators, and Representatives, it is a vicious teaching." [7] And as is well known, Justice Holmes, one of the most scholarly of the ninety-odd judges who have made so much of our law and determined so much of our national history and policy, asserted that the democratic political system of the American republic would still function even if the Court lacked the power to nullify Congressional legislation, something which obviously would not be true if it lost the power in relation to the state legislatures. But even Supreme Court justices may be mistaken about the nature of their function—and we have ruled out the argument from authority even if we perforce must admit the evidence or testimony of authority.

I

To prevent misunderstanding, I wish to stress that my concern with the question of democracy and judicial review is not primarily historical but analytical. I am a philosopher in quest of enlightenment—not a constitutional lawyer committed to a thesis. But where fundamental problems of policy are raised in a democracy about the administration of law, neither philosopher nor lawyer can claim privileged sources of insight beyond the competence of the reflective citizen. Historical issues are relevant to analysis of great problems of human affairs, partly because bad history is often the source of bad argument, but mainly because the wisdom of any proposal cannot be judged in a historical vacuum. To be intelligent about human affairs is to realize that we are dealing with historical and not geometrical phenomena.

I wish to take my point of departure from two acknowledged facts. The first is that John Marshall's interpretation of the *power* of the Court under the Constitution is now accepted as an authentic and integral part of the American political system. Whether it be considered right or wrong, whether it be a legitimate explication of a constitutional text or a rationalization to cover unconstitutional usurpation, John Marshall's interpretation of the power of the Court to nullify Congressional legislation has survived all previous attacks and criticisms. The second is that Marshall's *conception* of that power has been almost unanimously rejected today, as much by those who uphold and wish to extend the power of the Court as by those who wish to limit and restrain it.

Marshall's conception of what the courts actually do, of their nature and function, is expressed in one of his late opinions, in which he wrote: "Judicial power, as distinguished from the power of the laws, has no existence. Courts are mere instruments of the law and can will nothing . . . Judicial power is never exercised for the purpose of giving effect to the will of the judge; always for the purpose of giving effect to the will of the legislature; or in other words to the will of the law." [8] These words express a view of the judicial process which could make sense only on some theory of the general will, and which could be justified only on the undemocratic as well as untrue assumption that the judges, where questions are in dispute, know better what the will of the legislature was than it did itself. These are words which sound all the more ironical because they appear in a decision which boldly construes the apparent meaning of the language of the Eleventh Amendment to the Constitution into its opposite.

Were Marshall right about the *nature* of the judicial function, there would be little controversy about his claims for granting it such judicial power. But modern psychology, sociology, and legal history make far more plausible Holmes's concept of the judicial function expressed long ago in the well-known passages of his great book *The Common Law,* published more than eighty years ago.

The life of the law has not been logic: it has been experience. The felt necessities of the time, the prevalent moral and political theories, intuitions of public policy, avowed or unconscious, even the prejudices which judges share with their fellow-men, have had a good deal more to do than the syllogism in determining the rules by which men should be governed. . . . The very considerations which judges most rarely mention, and always with an apology, are the secret root from which the law draws all the juices of life. I mean, of course, considerations of what is expedient for the community concerned.[9]

If this is a substantially accurate description of the judicial process, it is apparent at once why judicial review should be of such burning concern to those of democratic faith. For if the Court is to serve as the keeper of the community's conscience, who is to keep the Court's conscience? The greater the Court's power, the more poignant the question. Concerning the Court's power there can be no reasonable doubt of its immensity, independently of whether or not one regards the exercise of that power as compatible with the spirit of a self-governing democracy. Nor can there be any doubt that its power has exceeded anything imagined even by those few of the framers who assumed that the Supreme Court would sit in judgment on the constitutional validity of the acts of Congress.

Of the power of the judiciary, Hamilton said in the *Federalist,* LXXVIII, in order to hasten ratification of the proposed Constitution: "It has no influence over either the sword or the purse; no direction either of the strength or of the wealth of the society; and can take no active resolution whatever. It may truly be said to have neither Force nor Will but merely judgment." On which Chief Justice Hughes, in the light of the history of the Court and his own experience, makes the appropriate comment: "To some, when the tremendous effect of its power of judgment in deciding upon the validity of legislative acts is considered, the statement appears to be almost ironical." [10]

I have said that I wish to eschew historical questions. But I cannot forgo a comment on the effort of those embattled partisans who defend the democratic character of judicial review to enlist Jefferson himself in their ranks. If they are justified in their concept of judicial review, they do not need Jefferson as an authority. To be sure, he lends the weight of a great name to a difficult position. But simple respect for historical fact and Jefferson's intellectual legacy should give them pause. Jefferson said several things about judicial review, not all of them compatible with each other. He was not so much concerned with denying the Court the power to decide the constitutionality of a law as with denying it "the exclusive authority" of such decision. This is the Jeffersonian and democratic sticking point. For unless it has the exclusive authority when conflict over constitutionality arises, it cannot be supreme in the sense in which it is supreme today.

Wherever a man's opinions have varied—and we are seeking, in justice both to him and the truth, to discover the view most representative of his position—the canons of historical scholarship require that we give the greatest weight to the views most frequently expressed. When these views have been advanced in the maturer years of a man's life while he is still in the possession of all his critical faculties, strengthened and enriched by experience, they have even a greater weight.

I shall content myself with reference to two letters—one to George Hay, the other to W. H. Torrance.[11] In the first, Jefferson explicitly instructs Hay to seize the occasion of Burr's trial to denounce the opinion of Marshall in *Marbury* v. *Madison* as not law but extrajudicial obiter dicta of which no legal cognizance need be taken. The chief ground offered for such denunciation is that Marshall has transformed a political system of coördinate powers into one in which the other two powers have been rendered subordinate to the judicial power. It is the second letter, the letter to Torrance, which spells out Jefferson's view in such detail that any doubts as to his mature views can be laid to rest.

... the ... question, whether the judges are invested with exclusive authority to decide on the constitutionality of a law, has been heretofore a subject of consideration with me in the exercise of official duties. Certainly there is not a word in the constitution which has given that power to them more than to the executive or legislative branches. Questions of property, of character and of crime being ascribed to the judges, through a definite course of legal proceeding, laws involving such questions belong, of course, to them; and as they decide on them ultimately without appeal, they, of course, decide *for themselves*. The constitutional validity of law or laws again prescribing executive action, and to be administered by that branch ultimately and without appeal, the executive must decide for itself also, whether, under the constitution, they are valid or not. So, also, as to laws governing the proceedings of the legislature, that body must judge for *itself* the constitutionality of the law, and equally without appeal or control from its co-ordinate branches. And, in general, that branch which is to act ultimately, and without appeal, on any law, is the rightful expositor of the validity of the law, uncontrolled by the opinions of the other co-ordinate authorities. It may be said that contradictory decisions may arise in such case, and produce inconvenience. This is possible, and is a necessary failing in all human proceedings. Yet the prudence of the public functionaries, and authority of public opinion, will generally produce accommodation. . . . But there is another opinion entertained by some men of such judgment and information as to lessen my confidence in my own. That is, that legislature alone is the exclusive expounder of the sense of the constitution in every part of it whatever. And they allege in its support, that this branch has authority to impeach and punish a member of either of the others acting contrary to its declaration of the sense of the constitution. It may indeed be answered, that an act may still be valid although the party is punished for it, right or wrong. However, this opinion which ascribes exclusive exposition to the legislature, merits respect for its safety, there being in the body of the nation a control over them, which if expressed by rejection on the subsequent exercise of their elective franchise, enlists public opinion against their exposition, and encourages a judge or executive on a future occasion to adhere to their former opinion. Between these two doctrines, everyone has a right to choose, and I know of no third meriting any respect . . .

Can anything be clearer? Unless additional evidence is forthcoming, should not this settle the controversy over Jefferson's meaning? *Either* legislative supremacy over Court and Executive *or* completely coördinate constitutional authority which would deny the Court power to nullify Congressional legislation—these are the only alternatives envisaged by Jefferson. To attribute to him any other view— no less the view which he himself denounced as "one which would place us under the despotism of an oligarchy" [12]—is a perverse and violent misreading.

Such a procedure would be comparable to maintaining that because John Marshall once wrote a letter, when he feared that impeachment proceedings would begin against him, in which he declared that it would be better for Congress to amend or reverse the Court's decision than to let the impeachment proceedings run their course—that therefore Marshall himself did not really subscribe to the doctrine of judicial supremacy. Writing in 1804 to Associate Justice Chase who was being tried in impeachment proceedings, Marshall observed: ". . . the present doctrine seems to be that a judge giving a legal opinion contrary to the opinion of the legislation is liable to punishment . . . I think the modern doctrine of impeachment should yield to an appelate jurisdiction in the legislature. A reversal of those legal opinions deemed unsound by the legislature would certainly comport with the mildness of our character than a removal of the Judge who has rendered them unknowing of his fault." [13]

The comment of Albert Beveridge, Marshall's twentieth-century Federalist biographer, on this letter is a mixture of apoplectic shock and incredulity. "Marshall thus suggested the most radical method for correcting judicial decisions ever advanced, before or since, by any man of the first class. Appeals of the Supreme Court to Congress! Senators and Representatives to be the final judges of any judicial decision with which a majority of the House was dissatisfied! Had we not the evidence of Marshall's signature to a letter written in his well known hand, it could not be credited that he ever entertained such sentiments." [14]

It would be absurd to judge Marshall's position by a concession wrung from him in a weak moment by a threat. And we know that the threat was quite real. Its existence is additional evidence of Jefferson's considered view, whatever its difficulties may be, of the role of the judiciary in relation to the other branches of government in passing on the constitutionality of federal legislation. The following passage from his *Autobiography* could hardly have been written by anyone who believed that the role of the Supreme Court should be what it actually is today.

It is not enough that honest men are appointed judges. All know the influence of interest on the minds of men, and how unconsciously his judgment is warped by that influence. [How like Holmes!] To this add that of esprit de corps, of their peculiar maxim and creed that it is the office of a good judge to enlarge his jurisdiction, and the absence of responsibility, and how can we expect impartial decision . . . I repeat I do not charge the judges with wilful and ill-intentional error; but honest error must be arrested where its toleration leads to public ruin. As for the safety of society, we commit honest maniacs to Bedlam, so judges should be withdrawn from the bench, whose erroneous biases are leading us to dissolution. It may indeed injure them in fame or in fortune; but it saves the republic, which is the first and supreme law." [15]

II

Just as I do not want to pursue historical questions for their own sake, so I do not want to lose myself in the minutiae of constitutional interpretation. Both are irrelevant to the main issue of what the democratic and desirable relation between Court, people, and Congress should be. I am content to accept the findings of Professor Edward S. Corwin and other scholars that the subject of judicial review of Congressional enactments was not a point at issue when the Constitution was adopted, and that different opinions prevailed among the Framers. But my conscience as a student of logic prevents me from accepting the extraordinary claim that the logical structure of the Constitution both gives the Court the power to nullify the acts of Congress in virtue of Article VI, Section 2, and at the same time gives Congress plenary power over the

Federal Courts including the Supreme Court by virtue of Article III, Section 2, Paragraph 2.

The first provision states that

> This Constitution, and the laws of the United States which shall be made in pursuance thereof . . . shall be the supreme law of the land.

On the assumption that the Supreme Court is the only agency which is enpowered to determine when the laws of the United States have been made in pursuance of the Constitution and when not, this would clearly give the Supreme Court the right to nullify acts of Congress with as much abandon as any advocate of judicial review could wish.

The second provision, after giving original jurisdiction to the Supreme Court in cases affecting ambassadors, ministers, consuls, and cases in which a state is a party, specifies that with respect to "all other cases before mentioned," which takes in quite a lot of ground,

> The Supreme Court shall have appellate jurisdiction, both as to law and to fact, *with such exceptions, and under such regulations as the Congress shall make.*

The phrases I have italicized empower Congress to remove from the purview of the Supreme Court's competence and authority any case in law or equity arising under the Constitution, any case in which it does not possess original jurisdiction. This provision, if taken seriously, would mean that the Supreme Court could be rightfully deprived of the power to review the constitutionality of any case or class of cases that Congress thought unfit or unwise for them to consider. One ardent advocate of judicial review—and of its democratic character, and of the beliefs that it was the explicit intention of the Framers to give the Supreme Court this power, and that a plain reading of the text shows this to be so—also maintains that because the appellate jurisdiction of the Court depends exclusively on Congress, "Congress can do pretty much as it wishes with the institution of judicial review." [16]

The best of heads, alone or in concert, occasionally nod. But it is psychologically inconceivable to me that the Framers were so muddleheaded or such Machiavellian jokers as to give the Court in one and the same document the power to nullify acts of Congress, and then give Congress the power to make the exercise of the Court's power impossible. It would be as if a man gave his wife the right to spend his money as she pleased, specifying that she could only spend those monies which he permitted her. The person who maintains that under this arrangement the wife really controls how her husband's money is to be spent, even when he leaves her without a cent, would be making the same kind of inference as those who infer that, despite the express reference to the power of Congress to regulate the Court's appellate jurisdiction, the Constitution gives the Supreme Court the power to nullify Congressional legislation. A coldly logical analysis of the provisions of the Constitution shows that not only has Congress the power to control the jurisdiction of the Court, except in a very narrowly defined class of cases, but that it has the power to set up special courts to adjudicate certain classes of cases and provide that the decisions of this Court should be beyond appeal. No document which intended to give the Supreme Court the power it presently has could have consistently contained these provisions.

The true state of affairs seems to have been that although the structure and logic of the Constitution clearly did *not* give the Supreme Court its present power, it acquired it during the latter half of the nineteenth century, basing itself on Marshall's reasoning in *Marbury v. Madison*. History, not the intentions of the Framers, or the propositional meaning of the "primary and sacred document," decided this issue. This is graphically revealed by the fact that today whenever proposals are actually introduced into Congress to limit the appellate jurisdiction of the Court in accordance with Article III, the most anguished outcries are heard by proponents of judicial review that such legislation is not merely unwise but flagrantly unconstitutional. It is true that at the time of the *McCardle*[17] case in 1868 Congress, with memories of the

Dred Scott[18] decision still fresh and smarting, passed a law removing from the jurisdiction of the Court any appeal on writs of habeas corpus arising from the use of military power in the formerly rebellious states, and the Court yielded. But it is highly significant that some outstanding proponents of judicial review now regard the decision in the *McCardle* case as bad constitutional law, and as one which the Court today would be unlikely to uphold.[19] And I think it unquestionably true that on this point they are right. Since the doctrine of *stare decisis* apparently no longer has any authority in constitutional law, the Court is not bound by any previous decision. What Chief Justice Hughes said about the meaning of the Constitution is literally true—every decision it makes *is* constitutional. Logically it can reverse itself; but it cannot really contradict itself.

If there were any doubts that Paragraph 2 of Section 2 of Article III of the Constitution has become an historically dead letter, it should be settled by the overwhelming reaction of the legal profession to the proposals made to Senate Bill 2646, introduced in the 85th Congress by Senator Jenner, to withdraw from the Court's jurisdiction five different classes of cases. Considered on their merits, those proposals could have been and were widely criticized. One could agree or disagree with the specific Court decisions which inspired this attempt to limit its jurisdiction, and still endorse Roscoe Pound's judgment that "the proposed legislation is unnecessary, and if enacted would be to a great extent futile and for the rest productive of confusion and altogether mischievous." [20] To say this is one thing—sufficient, one would imagine, to damn it. Altogether different, however, is it to say that the proposal itself violates the letter or spirit of the Constitution, that it destroys the American system of three coordinate branches of government, that it is "in the true sense, subversive of law itself," [21] or, in the milder words of John Lord O'Brian, "is so squarely at odds with our constitutional structure as to cast grave doubt on its constitutional validity." [22] These last observations express the firm conviction of most conservatives and liberals alike of the proper relationship between Congress and the Court. In the light of it, anyone who can believe that "Congress can do pretty much as it wishes with the institution of judicial review" can believe anything.

III

Let us leave historical and textual issues aside. What does an analysis of the actual structure and function of contemporary American government show when surveyed from a perspective that seeks to discover whether the three branches of the government are really *coördinate* in powers? This perspective is a neutral one, because those who strongly affirm the desirability of judicial review deny with equal conviction that this entails judicial supremacy in doctrine or in fact.

Let us imagine an anthropologist from another sophisticated culture who was making a report on the relative power of Congress, President, and Court in the light of the common commitment to the democratic faith. Let us assume that he bases his report not only on the text of the Constitution but on observations of American political behavior in the time of our century. It would be safe to say that he would discover the following scheme of checks on the various branches of government. Congress is checked by the existence of bicameral chambers, by the veto power of the Executive, by the nullifying power of the Court, and by the elective power of the people. The President is checked by the power of the Congress to override by a two-thirds vote, by the nullifying power of the Court, and by the elective power of the people. How is the Supreme Court checked? Its members, once confirmed by the Senate, are not removable for any decision they make. Although subject to all the influences which play on the minds of men, the Court's decision is not reviewable or reversible except by the Court itself. Formally and functionally this seems, on the face of it, to spell out clearly not a pattern of coördinate division among the three branches of government but, when conflicts arise, of subordination of the Legislature and Executive to the Judiciary.

Before concluding that this is so or that the Supreme Court exercises a *de facto* supremacy when conflicts arise, we must consider some indirect checks on the Court which are alleged to redress the balance, restore all branches to a coördinate status, and thereby preserve the democratic integrity of the political process.

(1) The Court may be checked through the process of Constitutional amendment. But this requires not merely a majority vote but an overwhelming majority. One-third plus one of the voting members of *either* house can prevent an amendment from being proposed. Once this obstacle is hurdled one-fourth plus one of the states can veto it. Thirteen states can exercise a veto on the will of the overwhelming majority of the population. In addition, the process is slow, cumbrous, and unwieldy in a world whose pace may require quick and decisive action. Further, the language of the amendment must itself be interpreted, and since the Supreme Court has the decisive power to interpret the meaning of the Constitution, there is no guarantee that the language will be read as those who drafted it understood it. Before dismissing this as a shocking supposition, it would be salutary to reflect on the fate of the Eleventh Amendment, which clearly prohibits a foreign citizen from suing a State but which was so interpreted by Marshall as to permit suits against the officers of a State.[23] More notorious and fateful was the reading of the due process clause in the Fourteenth Amendment, adopted after the Civil War to protect the rights of Negroes. The Court, instead of employing the amendment to *sanction* legislation in this direction when challenged, invoked it to prevent the states from protecting the rights of labor, white as well as Negro, by humane regulations of wages, hours, and working conditions. In discussing these and other illustrations of judicial expertness in *l'éxplication des textes,* Morris R. Cohen points out:

The people recalled the Court's decision of 1895 when they empowered Congress to tax incomes from *whatsoever source derived.* Nevertheless, the Court did not allow the taxing of incomes

79

from child labor and other sources, thus creating a privileged class free from taxation. The words from *whatsoever source derived* are as plain as words can be, but the Courts pay more attention to obsolete political theories and Marshall's dictum that the power to tax is the power to destroy—a dictum, however, which they disregard when they allowed Congress, through heavy taxation, to drive out oleomargarine and States notes.[24]

That some of these readings have subsequently been overruled by others in no way impugns the conscientiousness with which all of them have been made. Nor does it provide assurance that the text either of a Congressional enactment or of a constitutional amendment will be construed as the lawmakers intended. In recent times, the privilege against self-incriminating testimony guaranteed by the Fifth Amendment has been interpreted by the Court with such a latitude that it has been safely invoked by racketeers and conspirators in refusing to reply to pertinent questions, truthful answers to which, by no reasonable stretch of a sober mind, could hardly have incriminated them in a criminal case.[25] Whether one approves or disapproves of these wondrous feats of verbal prestidigitation is immaterial to the argument. They are conclusive, however, in showing that no Constitutional amendment can bind any Court which has the last word in interpreting its meaning.

(2) A second check is the power of Congress to appoint more justices to a recalcitrant Court. This action, as the fate of the Court-packing plan of Roosevelt indicated, always appears as an arbitrary procedure through which by fiat Congress imposes its will on the legitimate protectors of the Constitution. It is an action that may be subject to judicial review and rejection, depending upon the circumstances in which such legislation is carried out. Although accepted in the past, and even then widely felt as a *coup de main* during the days of Reconstruction, the emergence of the spirit of activism in the modern Court might find little difficulty in justifying the rejection of a similar proposal adopted with such transparent intent. In a certain sense the Court has always been packed by the Executive power, but gradually and not at

one political swoop. But as far as principle is concerned, the justices who are appointed in expectation that they would carry out a mandate to reverse a previous decision are still independent; they are still formally and actually responsible to no one but themselves. Once appointed, they cannot be controlled. When the Court attains its full complement, whether it be seven or fifteen, deadlocks may recur once more because of its power of nullification. It is hardly conceivable that in such situations the number of justices would be indefinitely increased on an assembly-line pattern to implement the legislative or executive will. Roosevelt's Court Reform Bill of 1937 was presented as a measure designed to prevent delays and inefficiency in the administration of justice, and contained some provisions which were subsequently adopted. But it was the measure proposing the gradual appointment of new justices which provoked national outcry and led the Senate Judiciary Committee to recommend its rejection with unexampled rhetorical vigor. Its report concluded with a statement which shows why the power of Congress to appoint more justices to the Court cannot be considered a serious check: "It is a measure which should be so emphatically rejected that its parallel will never again be presented to the free representatives of the people of America."

(3) There is, thirdly, an entire class of limitations on judicial review. The Court cannot take jurisdiction over everything, even within the purview of its powers. A genuine case must be brought before it. The plaintiff must show that he has a genuine "personal interest" in the case. If the case can be decided on other grounds, the question of constitutionality is evaded or postponed. One can pile up many of these restrictions upon the power of judicial review and make them seem quite impressive, but they have little weight when balanced by the indisputable fact that all these limitations are self-imposed. The Court has the power to take any case brought before it—any four judges have the privilege of granting a writ of certiorari. And it would be a badly schooled attorney who could not make out a plausible case for such a writ. The Court can find an indirect personal interest present,

since anything can be claimed to be relevant to anything else in social affairs, even if it is not present to lower judicial eyes. It can discover a great constitutional issue in a matter as trivial as the appointment of a Marbury, which Jefferson rightly claimed could have been decided on other grounds. It can create a constitutional issue, as it did in the *Dred Scott* decision by gratuitously outlawing the Missouri Compromise in a case which could have been decided by simple affirmation of the decision below without raising the issue, thus upholding Dred Scott's status as a free man but not acknowledging the right of the Federal Circuit Court to take jurisdiction in his case. To what it discovers and what it creates as a constitutional question, legally there is no one to say "nay." The very power to interpret a legislative act is the power to create a constitutional issue. The logic of the situation somewhat resembles belief in papal infallibility. The Pope is infallible in matters of faith and morals but not in matters which fall outside his sphere. But on some interpretations of the doctrine, the Pope himself is the infallible judge of what falls within the sphere of faith and morals and what falls without. If he himself determines the conditions under which he is speaking ex cathedra, this makes the area in which he can claim infallibility rather indeterminate. Those who call our attention to the many limitations of this type on the power of review seem similarly reluctant to acknowledge that the Court is the sole authorized interpreter of these limitations.

(4) The fourth limitation on the power of judicial review is the subjection of the justices to the Congressional powers of impeachment. But since they cannot be impeached for the performance of their duties as they see them but only for treason, bribery or "other high crimes & misdemeanors," this curb which applies to the legislators, and chief executive of the nation as well, does not speak to any constitutional issue. In passing, it should be noted that there exists no statute, Court rule, or decision which prescribes the grounds on which a justice is disqualified from participating in any case. Each individual justice is the keeper of his own conscience with

respect to the propriety of his sitting or voting in a case before the Court. This would tend to lead to the automatic dismissal of any petition for a rehearing of a case on the plea that one or more justices were disqualified because of previous involvement in the case at issue, despite the fact that the absence of a rule governing grounds of disqualification has led to some notorious quarrels in the sacred precincts of the Court.[26]

(5) The final limitation on judicial review I mention reluctantly. I do so only because it has been cited to mitigate the significance of the fact that those who are so powerful in determining social policy in a democracy enjoy life tenure and that, regardless of their physical and mental condition, their withdrawal depends only upon their own uncertain will. The justices, we are told, *are subject to control even though* they sit for life. They are inexorably controlled by death![27] True, but this is a macabre irrelevance. Death may strike down a justice. It does not strike down his decision. Death may strike down even the bloodiest of tyrants. This hardly makes it an instrument of democratic control, for unfortunately death is no respecter of democrats either.

Let us grant without further argument that our assessment of the comparative checks on the decisions of government establishes that judicial power is not unlimited. But it is just as obvious that the power of the governmental divisions are not coördinate, and that in the constellation of forces which make up American political life it is the other branches of government which are clearly subordinate to the Court when conflict arises.

The plain facts of the matter are sometimes impugned by a play upon words which interprets the term "Supreme" as if it meant omnipotent rather than dominant. Of course the Supreme Court cannot do everything. Nor can the Supreme Being, according to Aquinas. Judicial supremacy does *not* necessarily mean judicial tyranny. It does not mean that the Court is *all*-powerful, that its decrees are immutable, that it is immune from the contingencies of life and death. Homilies on human finitude are no more relevant here than they are in the discussion of problems arising from the specific difficulties created by divided power and authority in any community. In any system of unequal power relations, the personality of those who wield power may make a difference of considerable importance to those who are subject to the power. In a despotism a Marcus Aurelius is better than a Caligula, a Stalin is worse than a Lenin; but the existence of a despotism cannot be called into question because it is relatively benevolent. Only when we move from the plane of description to the plane of justification does this order of facts become relevant. I am not implying in the least that the American system of judicial supremacy can be likened even remotely to historical despotisms of the past or present. The point here is simply that the changing composition of the Court does not of itself have a bearing on the fact of its power as currently accepted.

Further, criticism of judicial supremacy which is motivated by commitment to the processes of democracy or self-government does not necessarily contest—indeed, it may vigorously approve of—judicial supremacy within the hierarchy of government organizations extending from municipalities up through the states. This was the point of Holmes's observation in distinguishing between the double functions of the Court. And in his famous article, which is the fount of inspiration of the school of judicial restraint, James Bradley Thayer wrote:

But when the question is whether State action be or be not conformable to the paramount constitution, the supreme law of the land, we have a different matter in hand. Fundamentally, it involves the allotment of power between the two governments, —where the line is to be drawn. True, the judiciary is still debating whether a legislature has transgressed its limit; *but the departments are not co-ordinate,* and the limit is at a different point. The judiciary now speaks as representing a paramount constitution and government, whose duty it is, in all its departments, to allow to that constitution nothing less than its just and true interpretation; and having fixed this, to guard it against any inroads from without.[28]

As Thayer read the situation in 1893—and events since then have amply vindicated his reading—the scope of the claims of judicial supremacy embraces the coördinate departments of government as well as the subordinate ones. If this is so, they cannot be accurately designated as coördinate. The United States Supreme Court is supreme not only in relation to inferior courts and subordinate legislative bodies but to the other branches of government as well.

IV

Well, why not? And with this honest question we reach the nub of the basic argument. Granted that in historical fact and present practice the Court does exercise judicial supremacy over other branches of government. Is this not justified morally and politically in terms of the basic freedoms of inquiry and person presupposed by the very processes of uncoerced consent? Who is to protect the people from the despotic inroad of government, even of democratic and well-intentioned government? Who is to represent, and negotiate between, the great enduring values of liberal civilization in behalf of which good government exists and which are so often lost sight of in the hurly-burly of political life? Who is to safeguard the people's natural rights, whether these be considered absolutely or intelligently? As Justice Douglas frankly puts it,

The Judiciary is in a high sense the guardians of the conscience of the people as well as the law of the land. It is much further removed from the political arena than the administrative agencies or the legislature. It sits aloof and detached from the community, not subject to the stresses and political storms of the other branches. Its decisions are more apt to reflect tradition and first principle than political expediency.[29]

I shall return to the concept of the Court as the guardian of the conscience of the people, but in passing let me note that Justice Holmes, writing many years before with an eye on just such notions, responded: "It must be remembered that legislatures are ultimate guardians of the liberties and welfare of the people in quite as great a degree as the Courts." [30]

Meanwhile, as an interpretative aside, the meaning of Justice Douglas's words may not unfairly be made more precise. In the light of his repeated and passionate dissents, he surely cannot have intended to say that the Court as such or in its automatic functioning is the reliable guardian of the conscience of the people. He must mean that *he* and those justices who agree with him are the true guardians of the people. Else we must conclude that the conscience of the Court is badly divided—indeed, considering some of its startling reversals, almost schizophrenic. And as for the Court's reflection of first principles—it sometimes gives us too much of a good thing, as when seven different opinions based on seven different sets of first principles are written in such a case as the Steel Seizure Case,[31] revealing a spectrum of principled differences much broader than that expressed in the briefs of the contestants. However, in order to appraise the position under discussion in its strongest not weakest guise, I shall assume for the moment that the Court speaks with an undivided voice, and that justices, at the very least, are not more fallible than their fellow mortals in Congress.

This view of the role of the Court distinguishes between judicial *legislation* in matters of social welfare and judicial *protection* of the rights and freedoms enumerated in the Bill of Rights and other articles of the Constitution. It is conceded that the Supreme Court has no justification in nullifying the legislative will where social and economic policies are involved, since these are substantive issues for which legislators are responsible to the electorate. But it has a responsibility to see that certain procedures by which substantive issues are considered remain uncorrupted and not eroded by sapping and mining.

That this distinction exists between what I have called the strategic rights and freedoms and the economic rights and privileges bestowed or denied by legislation seems to me quite true, although it was denied by the Court in the 'thirties, when it was presumably, then as now, the guardian of the conscience of the people. It is not, however, a distinction which has constitutional warrant by virtues of the general language or any specific provision of the Constitution. Its warrant is the commitment to the idea of a democratic, self-governing community. Even if the Bill of Rights had not been explicitly added to the Constitution as a formal amendment, the spirit of the American experiment in government required that the general sense of its political maxims be accepted as guiding the processes of government. Even the British Parliament recognizes the distinction in general between strategic rights and others. The distinction was first explicitly recognized by Justice Holmes and formulated by Justice Frankfurter in one of his professorial tributes—both leading members of the school of judicial restraint:

> He [Holmes] was hesitant to oppose his own opinion to the economic views of the legislature. But history has also taught him that, since social development is a process of trial and error, the fullest possible opportunity for the free play of the human mind was an indispensable prerequisite . . . The liberty of man to search for truth was of a different order than some economic dogma . . . Naturally, therefore, Mr. Justice Holmes attributed very different legal significance to those liberties of the individual which history has attested as the indispensable conditions of a free society from that which he attached to liberties which derived merely from shifting economic arrangements . . . Because these civil liberties were explicitly safeguarded in the Constitution, or conceived to be basic to any notion of the liberty guaranteed by the Fourteenth Amendment, Mr. Justice Holmes was far more ready to find legislative invasion in this field than in the area of debatable reform.[32]

The recognition that there is a distinction between property rights and other human rights by itself does not take us far in answering the question as to where in any *particular* case the emphasis must fall. For the distinction is itself a complex and shifting one. The pre-1937 Court was convinced that property rights were human rights and, as human rights, just as important as civil liberties. Where it was mistaken was in its too easy identification of "shifting economic arrangements" with property rights conceived as human rights. Neither Justice Holmes nor Justice Frankfurter would deny that the possession of some personal property is just as much a human right as any that may be enumerated. Strip a man of his possesions, and the possibility of the exercise of his civil rights is radically abridged. The fact that a man can own a mimeograph machine or a typewriter is some assurance that he can make his voice heard in protest. The error of the pre-1937 Court was to assume that the human rights to property as well as civil rights were best furthered by the system of economic *laissez faire* which obtained for social property, particularly in the means of production, distribution, and exchange. It denied the right of a self-governing republic to tamper with the existing economic order on the ground that this entailed a threat to the strategic rights which had Constitutional protection, thus giving almost automatic Constitutional protection to the system of capitalism.

One does not have to accept either Spencer's *Social Statics* or Hegel's *Rechtsphilosophie* to recognize that what can be distinguished can be shown to be related, and that there may be important connections between social property and the power it gives and personal freedom. This has to be convincingly established in specific cases, and cannot be logically inferred from a set of economic dogmas. Laws which regulate the returns on a public utility or set a ceiling on prices and a floor on wages can hardly be construed as restrictions on basic personal freedoms. On the other hand, one can conceive of certain measures adopted by Congress which might result in a monopoly of newsprint and a consequent threat to freedom of the press. Certain administrative postal regulations concerning the size, format, and carrying changes for printed mail might radically affect the circulation of ideas. It may be that certain controls, governmental or private, over a man's job or livelihood and the power which goes with it may be a more powerful threat, over the long stretch, to an individual's freedom of speech than an occasional or episodic attempt to interfere physically with it. The Marxian insight, already intimated by James Madison, that property in the things which are required for other people's existence spells power over men, opens a thousand doors from the field of our primary concern—human rights—to others. But these doors open both ways. The pre-1937 Court saw in many attempts to restrict the exercise of property rights in a market economy a violation of the human rights of those who owned property, even if it meant no more than a restriction upon the power of the owner of a large plant to dismiss his workers at will. On the other hand, the power which ownership of social property gives to restrict the human rights of the workers—in which the possession of *personal* property is one such right—motivates those who take seriously the public welfare clause to curb that power by a variety of social controls or by provisions which facilitate the emergence of countervailing powers.

Conceive as sharply as you please the line of distinction between economic legislation which affects the complex of strategic human freedoms and economic legislation which does not and is concerned merely with differing economic arrangements. It is still within the power of the justices of the Court to draw that line in practice—whether with easy abandon or sober restraint. No one knows how they will do it and when. All that can be known is that the doctrine of judicial supremacy gives them, and justifies giving them, the power to do it, that in exercising this power the Court often acts as a third and superior legislative chamber, and that the extent to which it uses the power it has depends upon the changing composition of the Court, upon the backgrounds, philosophies, and personalities of the individual justices. No one can be certain that what has been called the "revolution of the 'thirties"—when Justice Holmes's recommendation that the Court refrain from passing upon the wisdom of social legislation was adopted—will not be followed by a "counterrevolution." All it would require is the appointment of a few justices convinced of the validity of

Professor von Hayek's view of the consequences of interfering with a free market economy.

And let no one say that this characterization of the Court as a third legislative body is false because it cannot initiate legislation. Its vetoes often have direct effects upon social policy every whit as important as if it did initiate legislation. When Congress initiates legislation to change a given set of economic arrangements, a Court veto is tantamount to a legislative act to retain or restore them. The substantive effects of the decision are more important than the form.

Nor can one be certain that the growth of judicial activism in the field of civil liberties in the last decade will continue. Despite Justice Douglas's contention that the Court "is more apt to reflect tradition and first principles," there is nothing in the theory of judicial supremacy which precludes its empire from being ruled more by chance than by legal principles established plausibly from precedent to precedent. Chance refers not to an uncaused event but the irrelevant intrusion of an extrinsic causal series on the order of logical expectations. Even before the rash of reversals broke out in the Warren Court, Justice Frankfurter warned his brothers on the bench: "Especially ought the Court not reinforce the instabilities of our day by giving fair grounds for the belief that law is an expression of chance—for instance, of unexpected changes in the Court's composition and the contingencies in the choice of successors." [33] I, for one, cannot see what the recent spate of five-to-four decisions has accomplished, as far as settling principles goes, that a well-made coin-tossing machine cannot do equally well.

But surely—one can hear the inevitable and proper rejoinder—the question of the role of the Court as the defender of the personal rights of citizens against legislative oppression cannot be teased out from purely formal relations between concepts. Away with logical subtleties and pettifogging distinctions! The nature of an institution, like that of a man, is revealed not by definition but by its behavior—by its history. What *in fact* does the long history of the Court reveal about the way in which the guardian of the people's conscience and the spirit of the law protected the citizen's personal freedom and the basic rights on which self-government rests? What does the record actually show about the role of the Court in protecting minorities from the dictatorship of the majority—protecting not the property rights of minorities but their freedom of speech, press, and assembly, and of the essential prerequisite of the whole concept of democratic self-government: that is, the right to vote?

In the course of its entire history, there were close to eighty occasions on which the Court held acts of Congress unconstitutional. There is hardly a single clear instance in which the Court struck down Congressional legislation which curtailed the strategic freedoms essential to the healthy functioning of democratic self-government, at best no more than a single case in which it clearly rejected Congressional legislation that made it more difficult for a minority to become by peaceful means a majority.[34]

So far as I know, this truth is not contested by most scholars of standing in the field of constitutional law. It is a truth which has the profoundest implications for our inquiry even when the Court is credited with some powerful, indirect assists in protecting minority rights. For if the current state of our civil liberties be deplored, then the Court is no more an effective protector of our freedoms than Congress; and if the state of civil liberties, taken all in all, is healthier today than it has ever been in the past, as I myself believe, then the Court cannot be reasonably cast in the role of a freedom loving David defying the Goliath of Congressional power. At best, it may be pictured as a sleeping watchdog whose presence keeps fearful marauders away. This is the gist of Justice Cardozo's argument for judicial review from "the value of the 'imponderables.' " "The utility of an external power," he writes, "restraining the legislative judgment is not to be measured by counting the occasions of its exercise . . . By conscious or unconscious influence, the presence of this restraining power . . . tends to rationalize and stabilize the legislative judgment."[35] True enough, but imponderables are hard to weigh, especially when there are contrary imponderables. The contrary imponderable here, as Justice Cardozo himself admits, is the tendency of the legislature, when the system of judicial supremacy prevails, to evade its responsibility in carefully drafting and deliberating upon laws and leaving to the hazards of judicial interpretation the resolution of calculated ambiguities. Madison's fear that the Bill of Rights would be merely a parchment barrier to a rambunctious legislative body intent upon trampling the liberties of the people underfoot turned out to be wrong, not because of legislative fear of the Court or because of courageous interposition on the part of the Court, but because of Congress's own sense of constitutional responsibility and of the power of the electorate to call it to account.

The history of the Court, then, for all the rhetorical tributes paid to it, reveals no shining case in which the radiant ideals of freedom and equality were defended against legislative onslaught, with one possible exception. On the contrary, its history is studied with notorious illustrations of betrayal of these ideals when Congress sought to implement them. I refer, first of all, to the *Dred Scott* decision, which, in the opinion of an amazing number of witnesses contemporary to the event, was one of the major causes of the Civil War, or one of the two main proximate causes of that conflict.[36] I refer to the nullification in 1883 of the Civil Rights Acts of 1875, in which Congress forbade the enforced practice of racial segregation in various fields as a violation of the fundamental rights of American citizens. It was this decision which inflicted the most grievous wound on the body of democratic American polity, which legitimized humiliating discriminatory practices against the American Negro, and prepared the way for the morally outrageous decision in *Ferguson* v. *Plessy*,[37] which inspired, among other consequences, legislation in some Southern states that had until then escaped the dark and invidious pattern of segregation. It was these twin decisions which gave the aura of legality to political immorality, which bestowed constitutional sanction on racism as if it were compatible with the legacy of freedom, and which over the years contributed to strengthening the feeling in the

South that the efforts to draw our Negro fellow citizens as
equals into the kingdom of moral ends were expressions of
lawlessness. Almost sixty years later, in *Brown* v. *Board of
Education*,[38] the Court sought to make amends, and reversed
itself with pitifully inadequate and illogical arguments which
suffer from comparison with the eloquent and logical dissent
of Justice Harlan in 1883 in which he sought in vain to uphold Congress's right "to destroy the branches of slavery
after the roots had been destroyed."

A sober and unbiased reading of judicial nullifications
of Congressional legislation will show that on the whole they
have been more clearly motivated by a desire to preserve the
rights of private property from popular demands for social
welfare and social justice than by a fervent belief in the ideals
of personal freedom and equality.

It may be argued in this connection that the Court protected civil freedoms interstitially rather than surgically by
reinterpreting Congressional legislation which was unacceptable to it. For example, the Smith Act, upheld in the *Dennis*
case,[39] was liberally construed—some say radically emascu-
lated—in the *Yates* case.[40] As a critic of the Smith Act, who
has urged that Congress amend the language of the law and
stress the organizational aspect of the Communist conspiracy
rather than its propaganda, I am not concerned to defend the
Smith Act against certain criticisms. But it seems to me a
highly dubious way of defending freedom to place arbitrary
constructions on the language of the act and to assert by a
fastidious selection of what is in the record that "there is no
evidence whatever to support the thesis that the *organizing*
provision of the statute was written with particular reference
to the Communist Party," and even less justifiably that the
word "organize," in the language of the act, refers to creation
anew. What this last finding means is that if one organizes a
conspiracy, he can no longer be said to be an organizer a few
years *after* he has founded the conspiratorial organization.
No matter how active the organization is, no matter how continuous its life, after three years, by virtue of the statute of
limitations, those who founded the organization cannot be

93

held accountable. Presumably to be subject to the reach of the Smith Act, the conspiratorial organization must be dissolved and reorganized periodically. Here we have no clear defense of civil liberties or a vindication of the First Amendment freedoms, but semantic legislation, in defiance of ordinary usage, as a preface to judicial legislation. And despite the dictum that the Court takes judicial cognizance of all matters of general knowledge,[41] it betrays an extraordinary naïveté about how conspiratorial movements actually function. It seems to me it would have been a more valorous thing for the Court to nullify the Smith Act, if it believed that basic civil rights were being violated, than to pretend it was doing no more than clarifying the intent and meaning of the Congressional decision.

Of course, when the Court reinterprets national legislative actions it may be a controversial question whether it is strengthening or weakening the structure of American liberties. One might defend the nullification or emasculation of legislative intent if there were clear indications that a particular piece of legislation would in fact deprive the people of the basic freedoms on which self-government rests. But, as we have seen, once we slough off the rhetoric of the prophets of doom, there have been no conspicuous cases of legislation of this sort since the Supreme Court acquired this power, whereas there have been some cases in which the Supreme Court nullified legislative action which extended the area of franchise. That Congress is capable of unwise legislation, in this as in other fields, is undeniable. But the Alien and Sedition Laws were not nullified by the Supreme Court but were permitted to lapse by Congressional inaction. Had these laws been passed upon by the Supreme Court, there is no reason to believe, judging by the practice of the subsidiary federal courts and the temper of the bench at the time, that they would have been nullified.

At any rate, indirect nullification by judicial interpretation is not the issue. Those who are firmly convinced of the desirability of the judicial power of outright nullification would never be satisfied to let this power be exercised by indirection, by the devices of recondite exegesis of the texts of legislation and the intent of legislators. For it is easier to override a far-fetched construction of the Court by supplementary Congressional legislation than it is to adopt a constitutional amendment.

The basic issue we are considering is whether the practice of judicial supremacy can be reconciled in principle with the philosophy of democratic government. Those who defend the theory of judicial supremacy cannot easily square their position with any reasonable interpretation of the theory of democracy. Their difficulty is apparent in the character of the justifications. Sometimes they vote the dead and hail judicial review—but only when they agree with the decisions of the Court—as an expression of the "abiding majority" without telling us who counted the votes of the dead and why a majority made up so largely of the dead should have authority over the living. Once it is acknowledged that, in reviewing the actions of the highest elective government bodies, the Court is inescapably involved in "value choices," then it is also admitted that it is functioning as an organ of power, and not merely as a court of law merely interpreting the value choices expressed in the laws by those representing the people. The recognition that the Court makes value choices for those to whom it is not responsible is a source of uneasiness to the defenders of judicial review. They realize that this power is far-reaching indeed, and seek to hedge it in against abuse by certain qualifications. These value choices, it is asserted, can legitimately be made only when they are "entirely principled, e.g., [when they] rest on reasons with respect to all the issues in the case, reasons that in their generality and neutrality transcend any immediate result that is involved." [42]

This does not take us very far. Every Supreme Court decision seems to the justices who affirm it as entirely principled, even when it seems to their dissenting brethren less than entirely principled. All are men of good faith and of the highest integrity. Even when they are unanimous, their decision, since they are only men and therefore fallible, may not conform to the criteria of entirely principled decisions. Here as elsewhere they alone are the judges of the legitimacy of their own decisions.

Even if we grant for a moment that in the exercise of their judgment they are always and completely correct, their power is patently incompatible with the assumptions of a democratic, self-governing community. For it casts them in the role of a body of Platonic guardians but one, unfortunately, not so carefully trained. Nothing more misleading can be said than that these guardians are the guardians of the conscience of the people or that they represent their will in the light of a second and higher thought. In 1848 during the struggle for European democracy against continental absolute monarchs, the popular outcry in Germany was "Und der König absolut, Wenn Er unseren Willen tut." The defenders of the democratic nature of judicial review of the people's highest legislative body are in effect saying: "Und das Volk absolut, Wenn es der Wille des Gerichts tut." The will of democracy should prevail when the Supreme Court says so! This is exactly how it appears to some scholarly observers looking coolly at the mechanics of power. "The Supreme Court," writes Lord Dicey in his famous work, "is not only the guardian but also at a given moment, the master of the Constitution." [43]

The term "people" is an abstraction but not an unanalyzable one. Its referent is clear. The people do not make the laws —and one can generate a great deal of innocent amusement by pretending that democrats believe they do. It is the representatives of the people who make the laws. In a democracy the people elect their representatives and get rid of them when the laws they make are unpalatable to the majority. We know what Jefferson meant when he said that the "people themselves are the only safe depositories of government," from which he derived in a democracy "absolute acquiescence in the decisions of the majority—the vital principle of republics, from which there is no appeal but force, the vital principle and immediate parent of despotism." [44] This faith in the people may be justified or not. But a genuine democracy can rest on no principle which contradicts it. That is why the modern defenders of judicial supremacy—since we are all democrats now!—strain themselves by heroic feats of semantic reinterpretation to acknowledge this faith too. But in vain! The logic of their position defeats their effort—a logic which found its appropriate verbal expression, not in deferential reference to the people, but in Hamilton's caustic remarks and in the words of Gouverneur Morris, who, in the course of the Senatorial debates repealing the Judiciary Act of 1801, blurted out the truth about his faith and those of his fellow Federalists: "Why are we here? To save the people from their most dangerous enemy: to save them from themselves." [45] It has been charged that it was the American Constitution which "put a hook into the nose of Leviathan" [46] and drew it into the still waters of civil peace, but this seems to me to misread the social and economic history of the time. The hook in the nose of the American Leviathan was placed there by Marshall, but no chain was attached to it before the efflorescence of American capitalism after the Civil War.

"To save the people from themselves" may of course be interpreted in such a way as to remove the offensive paternalistic overtones. It may be represented as nothing but a restatement of the imperative necessity of saving *some* people from the oppressive actions of *other* people, even when the others constitute Jefferson's majority. And we are back again to the rights of minorities, to which Jefferson was every whit as devoted as any civil libertarian. The question is whether in a democracy the rights of a minority are *necessarily* imperiled by a majority unless these rights are taken under *sole* judicial protection when problems of their limitation arise. In passing it should be noted that it was not the upholders of judicial supremacy who were the most insistent upon the adoption of the Bill of Rights as a condition precedent to the adoption of the Constitution. It is among the latter, and above all the Jeffersonians, that the firmest opponents of judicial supremacy can be found.

Some who uphold the power of judicial veto over Congressional enactments on the strength of their theory of democratic government go so far as to assert that to abolish judicial supremacy is to substitute the rule of the people—which is another name in their political lexicon for the rule of the mob—for the rule of law. To them the real issue in this dispute is the possibility of freedom and justice under law. The rule of the representatives of the people unchecked by a Court which protects the people from its own representatives, and therefore from themselves, is an invitation to rule by tyranny —the tyranny of the majority.

To all who talk this way—who call up frightful pictures of the martyrdom of minorities when, in the absence of judicial review, they are subject to the power of the majority, who feel that only a Supreme Court and not merely a legislature can guarantee freedom and justice under law—there is a massive and not-to-be-gotten-around fact which challenges their position. This is the existence and history of English parliamentary institutions from the time of the Reform Laws of the nineteenth century to the present. How can they, on the basis of their *principles,* explain the fact that, despite the absence of a written Bill of Rights, of a court to pass on the will of Parliament, the state of civil liberties flourishes to such a degree in England that it is often held up as a model to us? How is it that, despite the fact that the English citizen has no more freedom to say anything or publish anything than what, to quote Dicey again, "a jury consisting of twelve shopkeepers think it expedient should be said or written," [47] no greener or healthier pastures of political freedom exist anywhere in the world? It was not always thus, especially when Parliament was built on a rotten-borough system. But the broader and the more democratic the electoral base of Parliament has been, the more flourishing has been the state of English freedom. This remains true even if we acknowledge lapses and room for improvement.

Whatever answer is made to this incontestable fact cannot be one of principle. Those who relate judicial review and supremacy to the preservation and defense of individual freedom must descend from the high plane of theory to the dubieties of American history. They must argue either that Americans are ethnically so different from Englishmen or that their history has made them so different from Englishmen that they are almost a different political species, that neither in the mass nor through their representative institutions can they be trusted to rule themselves without the supervision of guardians with life tenure. Indeed, they must argue that Americans are different not only from Englishmen but from the peoples of practically all democratic countries of the world—since our system of judicial supremacy, if not unique, has been adopted by comparatively few other nations. This would take a lot of proving. Nor can they argue that the federal system necessitates the presence of a court empowered to nullify enactments of the supreme legislative body because other federal systems function quite effectively without it.

Most of the grounds offered for judicial review are general, not historical, in nature. Usually they start from recognition of the obvious dangers to civil liberties inherent in any democratic community in which majorities reflect public opinion. They then conclude that the only or best method of curbing these dangers is to empower the judiciary to veto the action of majorities in the interests of republican virtue. If the arguments were valid, they would constitute grounds for judicial supremacy everywhere and would presuppose that the dangers to civil liberty would thereby be lessened. Thus Professor Edmund Cahan, an eloquent spokesman for the position of extreme judicial activism, asks: "Where would we really find the principal danger to civil liberty in a republic?" and answers: "Not in the governors as governors, not in the governed as governed, but in the governed unequipped to function as governors. The chief enemies of republican freedom are mental sloth, conformity, bigotry, superstition, credulity, monopoly in the market of ideas, and utter benighted ignorance." [48]

If the history of the republics of the past is relevant to our judgment, these are not the only enemies of freedom, or even the chief which have been usurpation and abuse of power on the part of the governors. The governors, even if we include the judges among them, as the passage above assumes, have hardly been freer of the vices enumerated in it than the people whom they governed. Not uncommonly the moral ideas of the people have been more humane and tolerant than those of their judges. The great moral reformers of the law have rarely been the judges. Grant the elements of bestiality and depravity in the governed, they are not so likely to have the vicious consequences observable when they are found among the governors. For Jefferson, at any rate, highest among the chief dangers to civil liberty in a republic is usurpation—judicial usurpation—or in his oft-repeated phrase, "the tendency of judges to enlarge their jurisdiction." The history of the Supreme Court, from *Dred Scott* to the present—including the things it failed to do which it could have done—exhibits in conspicuous fashion the very vices listed as the enemies of republican virtue.

It is one thing to say that the institution of judicial review of Congressional action has historically established itself in the United States, and that it is even popular. It is quite another thing to say that that history could not have been otherwise and our democratic legacy preserved. It is even more gratuitous to say or imply that the historical is perforce necessary or reasonable. Hegel to the contrary notwithstanding, the real is not the rational; nor, unfortunately, is the rational always real.

This conclusion concerning the power of the Court to review decisions of Congress contravenes one of the key assertions in Judge Learned Hand's profound and courageous discussion of the subject.[49] He argues persuasively that neither the text of the Constitution, nor the historical presuppositions of the time, nor the theory of democracy justifies the grant of this power. On the contrary, he maintains that such a grant of power would have been a clear violation of the provisions for the "separation of power," at that time believed by many the essential condition of all free government. Nonetheless, he holds that what did emerge was the only practical way by which conflicts among coördinate and separate powers of government could have been resolved. The inference, then, that the Court wields this power authoritatively is based simply on his inability to imagine any other way of resolving these conflicts different from the way it now does. But one can easily imagine half a dozen ways of negotiating such conflicts, all of which would have provided for consultation and renewed deliberation between the conflicting principals, and which would have given the ultimate power to the representative body responsible to the people.

Despite the fact that Judge Hand sees, albeit reluctantly, no alternatives to judicial review of decisions of Congress, he seeks to hedge this power against arbitrariness with cautions made familiar by the school of judicial restraint. In his case as in theirs, the qualifications placed upon the power of the Court are really no guide to what to expect. If the statute in question seeks to resolve the conflicts in value out of which it arose by "an honest effort to embody that compromise or adjustment that will secure the widest acceptance and most avoid resentment, it is 'Due Process of Law' and conforms to the First Amendment." [50] And if not, not.

Until we have operational criteria for the application of all these terms, this is ambiguous counsel. Interpreted one way, the great bulk of legislation adopted by Congress at the close of a session, when the impatient desire to adjourn makes genuine deliberation appear mere filibuster, could be ruled out of Court as anything but reasonable and impartial. Interpreted another way, anything approved by Congress except when its members are inebriated would be acceptable. Judge Hand's engrained intellectual honesty leads him to admit the very likely possibility that when the Court vetoes an act of Congress, despite the exalted language in which its veto is wrapped, what it may amount to is that "taking all things into consideration, the legislator's solution is too strong for the judicial stomach." The health of a democracy should not depend upon the uncertain digestive capacities of the judicial stomach, but upon the habits, values, and practices of the community.

V

In what direction do democratic principles point with reference to the future of judicial review? The United States is not England. The theory of parliamentary supremacy which provides no place for judicial review, although unquestionably more democratic than our own, is not likely to appeal to Americans on psychological and national grounds. But democratic principles do require the recognition that what is called judicial activism vis-à-vis Congressional authority breaches the theory and practice of democratic self-government. Although the practices of the school of judicial restraint are more compatible with democratic principles, the *theory* of judicial restraint is unsatisfactory. For it cannot formulate a clear and valid criterion to justify its interposition. The activists do not need any criterion except their own reading of the language of the First Amendment to the Constitution, their own sense of what other rights are to be included among the preferred rights, and their own decision on the proper hierarchy of preferred rights when they conflict. Their brethren, who are prepared to accept all Congressional enactments except those that are *unreasonably* reached, cannot formulate an objective rule of reasonableness, and in the end must fall back not on what appears wise but on what appears possible according to their own view of reasonable. Their deference to the legislative bill is laudable, but it is a self-imposed deference with very elastic limits.

In these circumstances it seems to me that the best method of furthering the democratic ideal, on the basis of existing historical practice, would be to adapt the proposal made by Justice Marshall himself in his letter to Justice Chase and which brought such a startled outcry from Beveridge. The justices of the Supreme Court should continue to function as they have done in the past, but, with respect to Congressional legislation, their opinion should have nullificatory force only when it is unanimous. The unanimity rule would apply only to the statutes of Congress and not to the States. That this rule would have a restricting influence on the power of the Court is obviously true, but it mitigates the galling possibility that where constitutional issues of life and death are at stake, the vote of one man would be decisive against the deliberative processes of representative government. After all, we do not find it unjust or unseemly in a jury trial, where only one man's life or freedom is at stake, to require twelve men to reach a unanimous verdict. Why, then, should it be unreasonable to request illustrious minds, considering first principles, to reach a unanimous decision where great issues of national welfare and security are in balance affecting the lives and freedom of millions?

Attempts have been made to reduce this proposal to absurdity by postulating certain situations in which Congressional action would be sustained by an eight-to-one decision against its constitutionality. It is said that feelings of moral incredulity and outrage would be generated among those adversely affected by the Congressional measure on the ground that a large majority of the Supreme Court justices had voted against it. In principle, the same criticism could be made even if the proposal were modified and it required a vote of seven to two or six to three against the constitutionality of a Congressional statute to invalidate it. This reaction is of course predicated on the assumption that it is the function *solely* of the Supreme Court to determine the constitutionality of legislation, an assumption reinforced by complacent historical tradition. Were the proposed reform made, presumably in time the Court would not be considered the sole repository of constitutional wisdom. Jefferson's concept would gradually win greater understanding and acceptance. Members of Congress would be more conscientious in exercising their legislative functions in the light of their constitutional bearings, and not "pass the buck" on moot points to the Court. In such circumstances the count would be not eight to one against constitutionality, but one plus the hundreds of legislators plus probably the President in favor of constitutionality. Even if we added the votes of the legislators against the measure which, failing a unanimous decision against it by the Court, was permitted to stand as constitutional, the situation would appear less bizarre than the present system, which makes it possible for legislation approved by enormous Congressional majorities and countersigned by the President to be invalidated by the switch of one strategic vote, illustrated in current five-to-four decisions.

It is true that where a man's life or freedom was at stake, and was forfeited in consequence of an eight-to-one decision that a Congressional measure was unconstitutional, particular care would have to be exercised lest there be a miscarriage of justice to the individual. The Presidential power of commutation or pardon would be available to prevent this if the Court decision and opinion were sufficiently persuasive to arouse second thoughts.

Were such a change as here proposed made, the system of judicial review would be less democratic than it is now. If the fruits of the change as they developed in experience were satisfactory, and conflict between the Court and Congress did not develop on the scale witnessed since the Civil War, one might settle for less than what a principled democratic system would require—especially if further changes would create sectional strife. Personally, I should be prepared to go further in the event that the unanimity rule did not prevent serious conflict between Congress and the Court. I should favor an amendment incorporating Marshall's suggestion which would give Congress the power to override a unanimous Court veto by a two-thirds vote of all elected members in both houses. Under such a provision, differences between Court and Congress would provide occasions for great national debate, somewhat in the way in which differences between the Congress and the Executive do today.

The democratic decision is much more likely to be a right decision when it is an informed decision. An informed decision, hammered out in the give and take of public debate, would be closer to the second thoughts and reflective will of the people—whose conscience the Court would like to be—than the closed discussions of the Court's Saturday briefing sessions.

I conclude as I began. Democracy is not an absolute value. In certain situations and in certain historical conditions, its consequences may be so prejudicial to freedom of mind, social justice, and other civilized values as to make some form of enlightened despotism—judicial, philosophical, or religious—preferable to it. The postulate that men can govern themselves may break down under the burden of problems too great to be solved or when sizable numbers are crazed by hate. But so long as one professes Jefferson's democratic faith, one must intelligently expand, not contract, the democratic process. For if, despite Plato, there are no experts in wisdom, we can all learn from one another. As I have already indicated, I do not believe there are experts in wisdom. The thinker who provided the most persuasive reasons for not believing it was Plato himself—that great dramatist of the life of reason, as Santayana calls him.

After having established to his own satisfaction that only those who know—the philosopher or magistrate kings—have a right to rule, Plato argues in the Tenth Book of the *Republic* that it is not the makers or producers but the users or consumers of things who are the best judges of their value. In the last analysis this epitomizes the argument for democracy. The entire corpus of Platonic rationalizations, which have re-emerged in a new idiom today, is shattered on the truth of the homely maxim that only those who wear the shoes know best where they pinch, and in consequence have the knowledge, and therefore the right, to change their political shoes in the light of experience.

Not everyone knows when their shoes pinch—children and idiots and the mentally disturbed do not. That is why democracy cannot work in the nursery, or in institutions of the feeble-minded or insane. But most grown and literate adults are better judges of their true interests than are others. Deny this and one must fall back on the paternalistic view that the citizens are the perennial children and wards of the state. Deny this and one denies not only the faith of Jefferson but any rational basis for the belief in democracy.

3

Intelligence, Conscience, and the Right to Revolution

I N THE FIRST CHAPTER, I restated and defended the Jeffersonian theory of human rights in terms of the centrality of intelligence in both the political and moral spheres. In the second, I continued a defense of the Jeffersonian view that the authority of intelligence must be vested in democratic political processes and institutions, and cannot be delegated to any body, judicial or not, which has power but no commensurate responsibility.

In this concluding chapter, I shall discuss a cluster of problems which may be called variations on a Jeffersonian theme. The theme is the nature and limits of democratic resistance to democratic authority. My conclusions will not be startling —originality in this sphere is almost always a sign of error— but I hope they will be of interest. At any rate, I console myself with Justice Holmes's observation that sometimes the vindication of the obvious is more important than the elucidation of the obscure—especially when the obvious is challenged. Even tautologies have their uses when counterposed to absurdities.

In the summer of 1960, a Declaration concerning the Right of Insubordination in the Algerian War was signed and circulated in France by 121 intellectuals headed by Jean Paul Sartre. It came to the defense of Frenchmen, in the army and without, who were being imprisoned, tried, and condemned for refusing to participate in the war and for having given direct aid to the Algerian rebels. It asked and answered affirmatively the questions whether "civic responsibility in certain circumstances becomes shameful submission" and whether or not there are "instances when the refusal to serve is a sacred duty, when 'treason' means the courageous respect of the truth." The government responded by taking certain measures against some of the signers, ranging from indictment of a few to banning some literary and dramatic personalities from state-controlled radio, television, and theater. The Declaration of the 121 set off a series of manifestos and counter-manifestos, some denouncing the signers as "professors of treason" and some denouncing the government for proceeding against them. It was more than the usual Parisian brouhaha, because some asserted that soldiers and recruits had been induced by the Declaration to desert. The repercussions of the Declaration were felt abroad, and some intellectuals in Italy and the United States expressed their solidarity with the signers.

Shortly thereafter in Great Britain, Bertrand Russell and some other leaders of the Aldermaston marchers called for a civil disobedience movement in protest against the decision of the Tory government to continue the policy of nuclear defense armament, originally introduced by the Labour government.

In our own country, in several parts of the South, in consequence of the desegregation decision, agitators abetted by some local officials called for both active and passive resistance to the legal directives of the courts to integrate the schools. Some of them made use of the same kind of language and type of argument which Northerners who violated the Fugitive Slave Laws a century ago had invoked to denounce the Constitution as "a compact with Hell." At the same time, Negro and white students carried out widespread sit-ins and sit-downs, violating local ordinances with the widely expressed approval of principled democrats who felt they were articulating the democratic conscience of the country.

Considered as a moral problem, the question of justification of revolution is comparatively simple, once we disentangle it from the mystical notion that submission to the will of a divine ruler requires submission to the will of the political rulers on earth. Indeed, such a notion is incompatible with a moral position on the generic question of political obedience. In principle a moral position must allow for the desirability of political revolution under certain conditions, even if on prudential grounds some practical decisions are left open. This is true even for those moral positions which regard the use of force or violence as intrinsically evil and wish to reduce it to a minimum. They cannot consistently condemn revolutionary action against oppressive government if there is good reason to believe that the costs in violence and human suffering of such action, broadly viewed, are less than the costs of the continued existence of the government. The problem is complicated by the fact that not all resistance to the specific evils of a government are intended to be revolutionary. The evil, however grave, may be episodic rather than systematic.

There are certain kinds of situation in which resistance to government, even when felt justified, is not intended to be an act, or part of an act, of total revolutionary overthrow. Antigone disobeyed the law without wishing to destroy the rule of Creon in behalf of another political order. She may have even felt some interest in preserving his rule. Analogously, the problem faced by a democrat in violating laws of a genuinely functioning democracy is much more difficult to resolve than when the problem is posed as an abstract ethical one independently of the individual's own political allegiance. Tyranny is tyranny, whether exercised by one man or by many, whether expressed through the arbitrary decision of a power-crazed maniac or through the considered decision of a majority pursuing some notion of the public good. But the *limits* of tyranny—the point at which disobedience is undertaken, the point of no return when disobedience turns to open resistance—cannot be laid down without reference to one's own political commitment. That is why it seems to me to be unrewarding to seek some general or universally valid answer to the *political* question concerning the justification of revolution on abstract ethical grounds alone.

Our own government was born in revolution, and the right to revolutionary overthrow of oppressive governments is enshrined as a natural right in the Declaration of Independence. Almost every line of this document assumes the validity of the democratic premises of a self-governing community. Its language could hardly be used by those who accepted absolute monarchy or benevolent despotism or the rule of an hereditary aristocracy as legitimate. It is axiomatic that anyone who takes as his point of departure its commitment to self-government cannot *in principle* be opposed to the revolutionary overthrow of an oppressive and tyrannical minority government anywhere, although he may conclude in specific cases that the occasion and times may make such action unwise. That is why democrats can hail and even encourage revolutions in Fascist, Communist, and other dictatorial countries and, without the slightest inconsistency, take vigorous measures to prevent totalitarians of any variety from overthrowing genuinely functioning democracies wherever they exist.

Why do I say that although a democrat *in principle* is justified in overthrowing a dictatorial regime, he may forgo advocating it? There are a number of obvious reasons, some of which may be made apparent by considering different types of situation. (1) Democrats may not be sure that they have sufficient strength and popular support to triumph; they may wish to avoid a *Putsch* which, even if successful, would require that they impose democracy in a country from above— as in some South American revolutions. Since such governments, established by a *Putsch* or by minority groups which declare themselves democratic, are usually unstable unless they transform themselves into dictatorships, democrats may wish to postpone action until they have built sufficient strength or sentiment to provide a majority consensus for the act of revolutionary overthrow. (2) But even when democrats are convinced that they have the majority of the population behind them, they may have reason to believe that the outcome is problematic because of the potential power of repression from internal or external mercenaries, better armed and more ruthless than the supporters of the revolution. Some of my Polish democratic friends, with poignant memories of what happened in Hungary when the West stood idly by as the Soviet soldiers, on direct orders from Khrushchev, slaughtered the freedom fighters, say that although the overwhelming majority of the Polish people oppose the minority Communist regime, few would ever dream of launching a revolution. Coming from gallant Poles, this is highly significant. (3) Even if the outcome is unproblematic, and there is good reason to believe that the democratic revolution against tyranny will triumph, democrats may regard the cost of victory as too heavy and wait for a more favorable course while continuing an outer and inner resistance.

None of these situations in any way affects the validity in principle of democratic revolutions in oppressive nondemocratic countries. But the question we are now concerned with is whether they have any bearing on the right to revolution or disobedience in *democratic* countries. Is there any implicit answer in the considerations so far offered? What does traditional political theory say? When we differentiate the problem of resistance to democratic authority by believers in democracy from the problem of resistance to undemocratic government, we cannot find much of a guide in the traditional solution offered in political theory to the question of the nature and limits of obedience to government.

The traditional solution was one in which the processes of democratic self-government were offered as the only reasonable alternative between unacceptable evils. We may recapitulate the argument as follows: there is a truth about revolutions in history, recognized not only by ancient thinkers but by the authors of the Declaration of Independence, that men "are more disposed to suffer, while evils are sufferable, than to right themselves by abolishing the forms to which they are accustomed." They knew that revolutions and civil wars are often terrible events in history—until recently they produced more terror and suffering than most wars. Our own Civil War, in which comparatively humane conventions of conflict were followed, was the bloodiest of all wars until that time. Ernest Renan once observed: "Happy is a people which inherits a revolution: woe to those who make it." This wisdom is as old as the human race. Hobbes was wrong in believing that a state of nature is usually marked by a war of all against all: it is only after law has been established and then breaks down, fragmenting the center of authority, that something approaching a war of all against all is likely to result. It was this realization which accounts for Aristotle's view that it is better for a bad law to be obeyed than by disobeying it to have all law brought into disrepute.

But how bad must a bad law be before Aristotle's counsel of prudence becomes a support of insufferable tyranny? Suppose a people accept a bad law in hopes of being able to change it by petition or the appeal to reason, but find "a long train of abuses and usurpations, pursuing invariably the same object, evinces a design to reduce them under absolute despotism"—what then? Here we must answer, as did the authors of the Declaration: "It is their right" to overthrow such governments. There is a limit to the blessings of law and order if they become the law of the hangman and the order of the grave.

How can we tell what laws of duly constituted authority to obey or to disobey? The second traditional position, sometimes evoked by the first, is that we should obey laws which conform with our conscience and disobey those which violate our conscience. This would be a wonderfully simple solution if only the conscience of the people spoke with one voice.

But conscience, of all things, is an individual matter. One man's conscience is another man's abomination. There is hardly any important law to which some man's conscience has not taken and may not take exception. If it is conscience, and only conscience, which justifies a man in refusing to bear arms in defense of his country, why does not another man's conscience justify *him* in ridding the country of the first conscientious objector? If a man's conscience is the sole or sufficient authority for *his* action, how can it serve as an authority for *my* action, by what right can it deny, suppress, or ignore my conscience? The history of the deliverance of human conscience has shown that an indefinite multiplicity of actions, varying from the pitiless slaughter of harmless old women as witches to the odd refusal to wear bone buttons, has been justified in its name. On the other hand, some of our cruelest actions—and especially our neighbors' actions—seem to be accompanied by no twinge of conscience whatever. Some Biblical incidents, which outrage our moral sensibilities when we read about them today, seem to have left unmoved the conscience of even contemporary prophets. At any rate, if the law were to be obeyed only when it is authorized by our conscience, the result would be anarchy. And not the anarchy of the philosophical anarchists! Most philosophical anarchists quietly assume that there will always be a policeman on the corner protecting them from the ordinary varieties of anarchy, including unphilosophical larceny and worse.

How do we escape the dilemma between the acceptance of tyranny, on the one hand, and anarchy, on the other?

The traditional argument in favor of democracy is that it is a political system which enables us to avoid both horns of the dilemma. In a democracy the major policies of government rest directly or indirectly upon the freely given consent of the majority of the governed or their representatives. Every citizen who meets certain standard qualifications has a right to participate in the political process and to convince his neighbors of the justice and wisdom of the deliverance of his conscience. The hope is that in the course of the political process consciences would submit themselves *conscientiously* to public criticism and debate, and finally work out the reasonable compromises which permit those with different consciences to live and let live, if not to live and help live. Tyranny is avoided by virtue of the fact that when a law is considered unwise or unjust by a dissenter or nonconformist, and the means of inducing consent remain unimpaired, he is free to agitate for its amendment or repeal. Anarchy is avoided in that after the discussion is over, and the votes are counted, the decision of the majority is accepted and obeyed as law. To the question, then, whether anybody who accepts the principle of democratic self-government can believe in the right to a revolution in a democracy, the answer is obviously, "No."

I am saying something more, I believe, than what Justice Hand said when he wrote: "Revolutions are often 'right' but 'right to revolution' is a contradiction in terms, for a society which acknowledged it could not stop at tolerating conspiracies to overthrow it, but must include their execution." [1] In this *legal* sense of "right," there can be no "right to revolution" in any system. What I am saying is that in the moral and political sense of "right," democratic theory and practice would be self-stultifying if they admitted a right to revolution in a democracy because the *faith* of the democrat is that all morally legitimate demands can sooner or later be realized through democratic processes without recourse to revolutionary violence. To a democrat there is a presumption of validity in any law passed by democratic process, in the sense that it commands a prima facie justified obedience. Its validity is comparable to the claim upon the assent of an individual who accepts scientific methods as the most reliable way of reaching truth, of any conclusion reached by these methods, even if later in the light of additional evidence the conclusion is modified or abandoned.

But this faith in the democratic process may be strained to the breaking point. It may be strained in two ways: by extremely unwise or oppressive substantive action, and by procedural violation. By substantive action, I mean that a democratic community may by due legal process adopt a measure so morally outrageous that some individuals say: "No matter how constitutional, we refuse to submit to this piece of legislation and will fight with *any* means to overthrow it." This was the position of the extreme abolitionists in the North who were prepared to approve even of secession from the Union to bring an end to slavery. At a great public meeting in the 1850's in Boston's Faneuil Hall in which the Constitution was called "a compact with Hell," a resolution was offered which declared: "Constitution or no Constitution, law or no law, we will not allow a fugitive slave to be taken in Massachusetts." [2]

By procedural violations, I mean a situation in which the democratic rules of political process are so abridged that doubt arises whether the outcome does represent the democratic consensus. Here the objection to the procedural action usually follows hard on the disapproval of some substantive measure which was adopted or imposed by breaching democratic rules. We shall find this kind of situation the most difficult.

Positions polarize with respect to the morally legitimate mode of behavior incumbent upon the citizen of a self-governing community when its representative assembly, by due process, adopts a measure that seems violative of basic human values. One of these positions may be characterized as the position of absolutist democracy which holds that obedience to democratic law, good or bad, must be unqualified. It obviously differs from the position of Bill of Rights' absolutism which asserts that any law which violates any right in the Bill of Rights has no legitimacy. This is the position which Abraham Lincoln took in a famous address on "The Perpetuation of our Political Institutions."

Let every American, every lover of liberty, every well wisher to his posterity swear by the blood of the Revolution, never to violate in the least particular, the laws of the country; and never to tolerate their violation by others. . . . Let every man remember that to violate the law, is to trample on the blood of his father, and to tear the charter of his own, and his children's liberty. Let reverence for the laws be breathed by every American mother to the lisping baby that prattles on her lap—let it be taught in schools, in seminaries and in colleges; let it be written in primers, spelling books and Almanacs; let it be preached from the pulpit, proclaimed in legislative halls, and enforced in courts of justice. And, in short, let it become *the political religion* of the nation; and let the old and the young, the rich and the poor, the grave and the gay, of all sexes and tongues and colors and conditions, sacrifice unceasingly upon its altars. . . .

When I so pressingly urge a strict observance of all the laws, let me not be understood as saying there are no bad laws, nor that grievances may not arise, for the redress of which, no legal provisions have been made. I mean to say no such thing. But I do mean to say, that, although bad laws, if they exist, should be repealed as soon as possible, still while they continue in force, for the sake of example, they should be religiously observed. So also in unprovided cases. If such arise, let proper legal provisions be made for them with the least possible delay; but, till then, let them if not too intolerable, be borne with.[3]

This is a very strong statement; it denies almost without qualification the primacy of moral principle over any political or legal decision made by duly constituted democratic authority. It does not distinguish between degree or occasion. For most laws which come from legislative chambers and governmental commissions, much can be said for this attitude, despite the needless extremism of the language. The consequences of the widespread violation of the Prohibition Amendment, by making crime a way of life and encouraging a cynical attitude towards law enforcement, were far more harmful to the community than the arbitrary and unjust restrictions which this ill-considered amendment placed upon the sumptuary habits of American citizens. A foolish traffic law usually works less hardship than would its widespread flouting. An unjust tax is to be deplored less than a tax strike. But suppose it is a matter which touches deeply not merely one's conscience but one's *reflective* conscience. What then? The law may command an action which outrages the strong feelings of a minority whose reasoned arguments and protests have been ignored. It was a situation of this kind which confronted those citizens of the North who, although opposed to slavery, were willing to suffer it so long as they were permitted to agitate against it, but who refused to obey the Fugitive Slave Act of September, 1850.

Here is a characteristic passage from Theodore Parker which expresses a not uncommon response by a man of religion to Lincoln's demand that all laws on the statute books be religiously obeyed and enforced.

Let me suppose a case which may happen here, and before long. A woman flies from South Carolina to Massachusetts to escape from bondage. Mr. Greatheart aids her in her escape, harbors and conceals her, and is brought to trial for it. The punishment is a fine of one thousand dollars and imprisonment for six months. I am drawn to serve as a juror and pass upon this offence. I may refuse to serve and be punished for that, leaving men with no scruples to take my place, or I may take the juror's oath to give a verdict according to the law and the testimony. The law is plain, let us suppose and the testimony conclusive. Greatheart himself confesses that he did the deed alleged, saving one ready to perish. The judge charges that, if the jurors are satisfied of that fact, then they must return that he is guilty. This is a nice matter. Here are two questions. The one put to me in my official capacity as juror is this,—"Did Greatheart aid the woman?" The other put to me in my natural character as man is this,—"Will you help to punish Greatheart with fine and imprisonment for helping a woman to obtain her unalienable rights?" If I have extinguished my manhood by my juror's oath, then I shall do my official business and find Greatheart guilty, and I shall seem to be a true man; but if I value my manhood, I shall answer after my natural duty to love a man and not hate him, to do him justice, not injustice, to allow him the natural rights he has not alienated, and shall say, "Not guilty." Then men will call me forsworn and a liar, but I think human nature will justify the verdict. . . .[4]

This position was strongly condemned by a great many believers in constitutional democracy, especially by Justice Curtis, who was to write the dissenting opinion in the Dred Scott decision. And yet there is moral heroism in refusing to do the things which Parker describes which we would not like to see disappear from life. But how can a *democrat* defend such unlawful action? It seems to me he can defend it *only* if he willingly accepts the punishment entailed by his defiance of the law, only if he does not seek to escape or subvert or physically resist it. If he engages in any kind of resistance to the punitive processes of the law which follows upon his sentence of legal guilt, he has in principle embarked upon a policy of revolutionary overthrow. If he insists upon his moral right to overthrow the government because of its infamous laws, then he has abandoned the position of the principled democrat and must stand on God's law as he interprets it or on the moral right as he sees it. We may agree with him on the ground that we are both "God's angry men" come to bring his erring children to their senses, or we may, as secular humanists, speak up for human liberty against democratic power, but we cannot consistently do so on democratic grounds. Were the democratic process to result in laws which we regard as so morally iniquitous as to justify overt or implicit rebellion, we would have to conclude that men were incapable of self-government, that good government could not be achieved by democratic processes. To seek to overthrow a democratic government whose deliberative processes, attended by all the procedural safeguards of civil and political rights, results in a reign of terror against an innocent and helpless minority may certainly be morally justifiable. To do so in the name of democracy is usually a piece of suave hypocrisy or self-deception, and is to shift the meaning of democracy from a set of political procedures to a set of goals which might very well be achieved by other than democratic political procedures.

John Brown and others like him had the honesty of their fanaticism. They never pretended that they were violating and destroying the fabric of democracy in the name of democracy. For the history of democracy had shown them that justice, freedom, God's will—however they conceived it, mistakenly, as I believe, or not—could not be achieved by the democratic political process. They would have felt at home in a theocracy administered by their favorite sectarian luminaries. Thoreau, on the other hand, never saw the issue clearly. His theoretical position as expressed in his *Essay on Civil Disobedience* is thoroughly confused and muddled because it implies both that one can accept democracy as a political system and also believe that every citizen has a right to overthrow it if any law passed by a democracy violates his obligation to the right. Thoreau's practice was, however, compatible with the democratic position in that, refusing to pay taxes to be used to enforce laws he regarded as evil, he did not take to the hills but gladly and proudly went to jail. Under certain circumstances, if the penalty for the violation of a law were extreme enough, one can conceive a democrat violating the law and at the same time willingly forfeiting his life rather than weakening or betraying the structure of democratic law by flight or resistance. The argument which Socrates makes in the *Crito* is unanswerable and is binding on anyone who, despite his differences with the democratic community, still feels that he is a loyal member of that community and not at war with it. In war—national, civil or class war—one expects prisoners to attempt to escape. In Socrates' case, he carried matters a little far, not by his willingness to accept punishment, but by his insistence upon it. One gets the impression that he thought he was punishing the Athenians. And perhaps he was.

The situation is more complicated with respect to the violation of procedural principles of a democracy by its legislative or executive organs. For in such instances one may claim that beyond a *certain point* a democracy in violating its own democratic laws is moving into a condition of despotism which emboldens the democratic dissenter or rebel to proceed against it as he would against any despotism. According to some democrats, Lincoln violated the laws of democracy in suspending the writ of habeas corpus in states which were outside the immediate theater of war. One can conceive of many situations in which an unwise or corrupted democracy destroys its own institutional presuppositions. But so long as one still regards the community, despite its procedural lapses, as still functioning under a democratic political system, revolutionary opposition to it cannot be justified on democratic grounds.

It is at this point that we must recognize a distinction in principle between revolutionary violence and nonviolent civil disobedience, even though situations may arise which make it difficult *in practice* to draw the precise line. Although a democrat must condemn any kind of revolutionary violence, no matter how nobly motivated, he may condone, within certain narrowly prescribed limits, some forms of civil disobedience, Lincoln to the contrary notwithstanding. A situation may arise in which a democrat believes that a municipal or state law violates the fundamental law of the land. In a desire to test the local law—and it is a law because it is currently being enforced—a democrat may defy it in the way in which Norman Thomas defied the decrees laid down by "I-am-the-Law" Mayor Hague of Jersey City. Such situations are clear and simple. One may, however, go further. Even when such laws are upheld by the courts of highest instance, even in cases where federal laws have been held constitutionally valid, a democratic dissenter may, without inconsistency to his principles, disobey them provided he is prepared to accept the consequences. His justification lies in his hope that his act, and the acts of others, will serve as moral challenge and educational reinfluence on the attitudes of the majority. His very willingness to endure all sorts of hardships and their attendant deprivations normally arouses, when not compassion, second thoughts about the wisdom and justice of the law in question. That is why a sincere democrat who disobeys the law cannot whine or dodge or evade or fall back on the Fifth Amendment. Indeed, the very effectiveness of the violation of the law, in the intent of the dissenter, depends upon his being punished. Much worse than the punishment is to be ignored. I recall that during the war against Hitler, a group of conscientious objectors all crowding the age of sixty-five, led by Reverend A. J. Muste, publicly proclaimed their intention to defy the Registration Act. They gave up their valuable apartments, put their furniture in storage, made their farewells to their families, notified the newspapers—and awaited the federal marshal. But someone in Washington with a sense of humor or proportion completely ignored them. The expectant martyrs were furious, and spoke about the deception of the government in shockingly un-Christian terms.

Of course no one can lay down in advance at what precise point civil disobedience, especially mass civil disobedience, by disorganizing essential services, may lead to the destruction of the entire democratic process. This is something which cannot be settled by principled formulations. But any democrat who advocates or undertakes a policy of civil disobedience must take note of considerations of this order and, as a democrat, must always stop short this side of the line.

We must also qualify, in the interests of clarity, what was said above about the nonviolent character of civil disobedience. The absence of violence is normally evidence of the bona fides of those who publicly disobey a law, since it reveals the absence of revolutionary intention. But the judgment of the character and legitimacy of acts of civil disobedience must, in the end, depend not so much on whether the acts are nonviolent or not but on the consequences of those acts on the community. A nonviolent or passive act of disobedience which will result in starving a city or in deprivation of essential care may be much worse and less tolerable, from a democratic point of view, than a flurry of transient violence.

We are now in a position to apply some of the distinctions we have made to the situations from which we took our point of departure. On the assumption that Sartre and his group are democrats, and on the assumption that they are not merely expressing an opinion, the incitement to French soldiers to desert is incompatible with the existence of a democratic state if the Fifth Republic is considered democratic as most of the signers, but not Sartre, seem to believe. It is sometimes said that no government can tolerate incitement to desertion and insubordination among its military forces. This is an incipient revolutionary act. True, but that is not the point here. As democrats, we can see nothing wrong in inciting the soldiers of totalitarian states to come over to the camp of freedom. The question is restricted only to soldiers of a democratic state. Some of the signers have made loud protests against the halfhearted measures taken against them, and some of the extralegal sanctions invoked have, indeed, the touch of a French farce and an uncharacteristic logical inconsistency about them. There is also an air of *opéra bouffe* about the protests of some individuals against government sanctions on the ground that, although the government may have a right to shoot the signers, it has no right to prevent them from singing over the state-owned radio. Nonetheless, an important point is involved here. If the signers are guilty of incitement to desertion, they should be charged and proceeded against under due legal process. But *until* this is done, the imposition of other extralegal discriminatory sanctions against them cannot be justified, if they are not state officials bound by a code of professional conduct, for they have not yet been adjudged guilty.

One thing should be clear. If it is established that the declaration was an incitement to desertion and disobedience, I can see no democratic justification for protesting or refusing to accept the consequences of the violation of the law. One cannot with integrity—especially if one is a democrat—both defy a law of the democratic community, take bows and plaudits for a stand widely heralded as "heroic," and then run from the consequences of one's heroism. After all, a soldier who deserted on the strength of the appeal of these intellectuals might be court-martialed and shot. How can those who issued the appeal to him responsibly claim immunity for actions which their appeal brought about?

The discussion precipitated by the case of the French intellectuals revealed some curious—even startling—misconceptions about the nature of democracy by individuals who regard themselves as committed to democratic principles. In a supporting statement drawn up by some Italian intellectuals, which was endorsed by some of their American confreres, it was asserted that "The right to disobedience . . . is the essence of democracy. It is an extreme right, to be exercised only in extreme circumstances." [5] The inadequacy of this radical political innocence is apparent on its face. A strange essence, this right to disobedience! The essence of anything is found, not in extreme circumstances, where it is difficult to tell whether we are dealing with a phenomenon which belongs to the class whose essence we are defining, but in its normal and ordinary state. As well say that the essence of humanity is to be found in the extreme, borderline cases in which we do not know whether to classify an animal as belonging to Homo sapiens or to the lower primates. To make the right to disobedience "essential" to democracy is to conceive of democracy as a state of permanent civil war, except possibly on the assumption that men have angelic natures, so that their disagreement with the decisions of the majority never goes beyond the limits of philosophic discourse. But not even the "real" angels of sacred theology, judging by the story of Lucifer, are that angelic!

In explaining what he means by this peculiar concept of the essence of democracy, the author of the supporting Declaration, Nicola Chiaromonte, writes: "The principle of disobedience . . . is implicit in the very essence of democracy in the sense that, if democracy rests on an ever renewed act of *spontaneous* obedience to law, the moment the act becomes in all conscience impossible, is also the moment both of revolt and of the end of democracy." [6]

This is false and horrendous doctrine. It logically implies that a democracy is impossible unless it rests on unanimous and spontaneous obedience to law. If such a situation existed, we should have no need of the state or of laws with any penal sanction whatsoever. A democracy rests upon the freely given consent of the majority of the governed, after full, fair, and free discussion and criticism. The obedience to the laws of a democracy by a democrat need not be spontaneous in the least. It can be as reluctant as one pleases, so long as they are obeyed—with the exception of the carefully circumscribed acts of civil disobedience. The Spanish Loyalist government was no less democratic because Franco regarded revolt against it as a matter of conscience. Signor Chiaromonte, like so many other well-intentioned persons—whether Christian or humanist, anarchist or pacifist—assumes that only men of good faith have consciences, and that by definition the conscience of all men of good faith is at least compatible with, if not the same as, his own.

The instance of the conscientious objector to war is more familiar to us. Those who oppose *any* kind of war on religious grounds do not feel bound by any overriding commitment to the values of democracy, even in situations where democracy can survive only by means of a defensive war. They feel about war—any war—the way John Brown felt about slavery, but happily, unlike John Brown, they cannot consistently engage in any violent action in behalf of their cause. Modern democracies try to accommodate these religious dissenters as much as possible by giving them an opportunity to perform nonmilitary service. Where any kind of service is refused, they may be held accountable if their refusals are too widespread and dangerous to be ignored and the prospects of democratic survival weakened. It is—or should be—one of the great merits of democratic government that it respects and tries to accommodate *as far as possible* the scruples of those who believe that their relation to God "involves duties superior to those arising from any human relation," but, as we have seen, we cannot absolutize this belief. As democrats we cannot suffer it to go beyond the line set by reflective morality and the necessity of safeguarding the whole structure of other democratic freedoms.

The instances of nonreligious violators of laws and obligations relating to military defense should be treated no differently, if their moral convictions against any war are sincere. To the extent that they are principled democrats, we can rely on their setting limits on the scale of their own civil disobedience. This may not be true for some groups who are engaging in the practice of civil disobedience in behalf of unilateral disarmament and who are prepared, however reluctantly, to sacrifice free institutions to the risk of a nuclear war in their defense. Since, in the extreme situation posed by the threat of war, they are disposed to surrender democracy, they may be tempted to encourage the transformation of a movement of civil disobedience into one of revolution if this were the only means which seemed available to prevent war. For this reason nonpacifist civil disobedience movements are as a rule far more dangerous than purely pacifist ones.

Those who are currently engaged in violating the federal laws relating to desegregation in education are probably not very much concerned whether their behavior is consistent with democratic principles or not. To the extent that this opposition is articulate, one gathers that some Southern editors and political figures believe that in resisting the law they are upholding the Constitution against the Supreme Court. The ruffians who have been threatening parents willing to send their children to desegregated schools are something else again. The law must be enforced against them. But enforcement, although necessary, is not enough. If disorders continue, they cannot be attributed exclusively to agitators but to principled resentment against the law. The task of the over-all democratic community is to convince those who feel that they are fighting *for* democracy in fighting *against* the law, that they are mistaken in this belief and that the spirit of democratic community, whose basic principle is equality of concern for all individuals to develop themselves as persons, requires the abandonment of unjust and arbitrary discriminations against any group of citizens.

The sit-in and sit-down strikes of students, since they have not been accompanied by violence and since they have ended happily in some Southern towns and cities, are the best illustrations of a kind of civil disobedience undertaken in the name of democracy to reëducate a community to the significance of the democratic way of political life. It may be that those who yielded did so out of convenience or business considerations. No matter. Habit, use, and wont will gradually put down taproots to nourish the frail blossoms of social equality which until now have withered in the climate of hate and fear. Nonetheless, it must be acknowledged that civil disobedience is at best a danger to a democracy, even when in small doses it may have some healthy medicinal effect. It can be legitimately undertaken only when the action is sustained by a great moral principle implicit in the democratic process, and only when there is no great danger it will be a preface to riot and civil war, or imperil the functioning of democratic political life.

There is such a thing as social timing in human affairs. Properly regarded, it enables one to strike a blow for human liberation which will echo in the hearts and minds of even those against whom it is directed. If social timing is disregarded, then, no matter how exalted the motive behind the action, it may shatter all bonds of community and have disastrous effects upon the cause of freedom. A half-century ago, the Southern sit-ins and sit-downs would have resulted in a series of bloody disasters. What Gandhi accomplished against the British could not have had the same effect at the time against a Nazi or Communist or Japanese military regime, because British democracy had already reached a point where its colonial possessions troubled the sensibilities and conscience of its citizens.

One may contrast the civil disobedience of the sit-in and sit-down strikes against racial segregation in the United States with the kind of sit-in and sit-down strikes conducted by the left-wing Socialist party of Japan in recent years. Seizing upon the phrase "the dictatorship of the majority," from some misremembered context in the lessons of their American teachers of the Occupation, and fearful of the fancied consequences of legislation proposed by the majority party in the Japanese Diet, they mobilized their partisans time and again to prevent the speaker from opening the session and by locked-arm tactics prevented the ministers and leading members of the opposing party from attending to their legislative functions. Even if their grievances had been legitimate, and their fears of unwise legislation justified, by their tactics they did far more damage to the faltering, uncertain traditions of democratic process in Japan than what would have resulted from the enactment of the measures they proposed. We must therefore distinguish between the tactic of civil disobedience as part of a calculated strategy to destroy the political democratic process—Communists too pose as pacifists and civil libertarian absolutists!—and civil disobedience undertaken with a kind of religious veneration for the values of democracy and which inspires by its openness and self-sacrifice community rethinking of the issues involved.

All this may strike enthusiasts, who identify good causes only with their own causes, as hedging the right to civil disobedience about with too many restrictions and cautions to make it a powerful means of social protest and change. But I submit that democratic theory requires that these limitations be put upon it, whereas common sense tells us that the effectiveness of civil disobedience in raising the standards of democratic practice is, beyond a certain point, inversely proportional to its frequency.

Lest I be misunderstood, I should like to repeat that nothing I have written about civil disobedience implies that there is an obligation on the moral and religious dissenter to accept the authority of the political system of democracy blindly, to forgo his moral claims to defy the entire structure of the democratic ethos on the grounds that it imperils some sacred value or some assurance of salvation which for him is beyond price and commands an *unpostponable* allegiance. In other words, if individuals refuse to play within the rules of the democratic game on the ground that these rules are too frivolous for the great stakes at issue, they are free to act as if they are at war with the democratic community. By the same token, democrats are just as free to crush them if they resort to war instead of argument. Despite Lincoln's words in praise of democracy as a political religion, his moral sensibilities rejected the absolutism which makes a fetish of any set of political institutions independently of their fruits. Facing the grim threat of rebellion which he believed both politically and morally unjustified, he nonetheless acknowledged in his First Inaugural, "If by the mere force of numbers a majority should deprive a minority of any clearly written constitutional right, it might in a moral point of view justify revolution—certainly would if such a right were a vital one."

I am not asserting that in such historical situations of conflict, when conscience is arrayed against conscience, both sides are equally justified merely because they stake their lives on the outcome. One or another side may be hasty, partial, or mistaken about what their needs and interests are, and the consequences of the different methods of gratifying them. The faith of the democrat in this juncture of disagreement is one with the faith of all liberal civilization. It is that so long as the processes of reflective inquiry are kept open, what seems to be an ultimate or inarbitrable conflict of interest and value may prove to be negotiable—at the very least, that mutual agreement can be established that there are some lesser evils in the situation which are preferable to the risks of mutual destruction. If and when such conflicts are not negotiable, if it is true that the reflective good of one side is incompatible with the reflective good of the other, what is shown is *not* that the moral values at issue are devoid of objectivity but that they lack universality, not that they are relativistic, in the sense that they are arbitrary and subjective, but that they are relational—that is to say, related to the kind of creatures we are or may become.

At any rate, whether the alleged antinomies of "ultimate" moral conflict can be resolved by this theory of objective relativism, the freedom or liberty which is inherent in the theory and practice of democracy is not the liberty to do anything one's conscience dictates. A surprisingly large number of generous spirits have been misled by this notion. No less a thinker than Lord Acton, in his *History of Freedom*, gives currency to this illusion of noble but naïve minds. He writes: "Liberty is the assurance that every man shall be protected in doing what he believes his duty, against the influence of authority and majorities, custom and opinion." [7] This would entail our protecting the actions of madmen and fools, and invite perpetual war between conflicting fanaticisms. The only duty which can make a legitimate claim to overarching authority in a democratic community is the duty to accept the test of all the rational methods that can be brought to bear on our value claims.

These value claims may be legion, and when intelligence

tests them, it can only do so in the light of commonly shared values which grow out of common interests. Although these too may be questioned at any given time they possess the working authority of experience. None is final. A democratic society is more congenial than other societies to the recognition of a plurality of values. It is also more vulnerable than other societies in virtue of the potential conflicts latent in such plurality. That is why the perpetuation of the rationale of the democratic process becomes of primary importance to all who cherish the ideal of an open society with plural values, even when they differ among themselves concerning the order and hierarchy of values. Religious freedom was originally born as a consequence of the impotence of religious persecution. But, once having tasted the fruits of religious toleration, even the believer in the "true" religion—whatever it may be —is likely to accept religious freedom as intrinsically justified and not merely as a hedge against possible persecution or as a means of converting unbelievers.

There is a corresponding moral extension—not displacement—from individuals and individual values to society when it is considered as a set of arrangements which nurtures and cherishes individuals and individual values. The good life cannot be pursued independently of the good society because a bad society can make the good life impossible. Failure to recognize this sometimes leads to very strange pronouncements. Consider, for example, the avowal of E. M. Forster that "if I had to choose between betraying my country and betraying my friend, I hope I should have the guts to betray my country." [8]

This paradoxical remark is Forster's way of saying that personal relations should come first in the order of our moral allegiances, and that social and political systems are ultimately to be tested by the character of the personal relations they make possible and not by production figures, rates of economic growth, and the mythologies of progress. To the extent that a democracy is truly committed to an equality of concern for all human beings to develop themselves to the fullest reach of their personalities, it is the faces which men turn to their neighbors in everyday life which carry the message of their faith rather than the cold and remote promises of their ideology.

Taken unqualifiedly, however, Forster's remark violates the very spirit which he strove to articulate. Surely his dictum does not apply to any country, any friend. Suppose the country a democracy, worthy of the two cheers which is top score for Forster for anything short of the City of God or brotherly love. Suppose the country a democracy which regards the individual as possessing intrinsic worth, and which views the quality of personal relations as the test of all social institutions. Suppose the country a democracy which encourages variety and permits criticism. Does this not make an enormous difference to the decision of which to betray—country or friend? And suppose one's friend—something hard to imagine but conceivable—turns out to be a Quisling, a Fuchs, a Hiss, prepared to open the gates of the open society to its deadly foes—foes of every value Forster holds dear. Would Forster still pray to have the guts to betray his country rather than his friend? I very much doubt it. In betraying his country he would be betraying many more friends, who are no less deserving of his concern, than the one who creates the dilemma. Nor is it necessary to paint countries in black-and-white contrasts to recognize that it is the direction in which they are moving which counts.

The days of Epicurus, who could cultivate his friendships and his garden in independence of the world, are gone forever. There is no longer any distinction between Greek and barbarian. We are all Greeks, and underlying all other differences is whether we are to live in a free society or a totalitarian one. To profess an indifference to the good society in behalf of the pursuit of the good life for ourselves and our friends indicates an indifference to the lives of others which is sure to be revenged upon us and our descendants. It is not necessary, even if it were possible, to love all men, but in a democracy it is necessary to respect every man until he forfeits our respect.

This poses for us the last great problem. Its theoretical roots are as tangled and deep as its practical sweep is troublesome and wide. What attitude should the democratic community take toward political groups which invoke democratic rights and privileges in order to destroy the entire system that makes these rights and privileges possible? What action, if any, should a democratic community take toward any minority that proposes, if and when it comes to power, to make forever impossible the opportunity of any other minority to become a majority through peaceful and orderly means, by destroying all the rights of the Bill of Rights and instituting a reign of terror?

This problem is posed in a unique way by twentieth-century totalitarianism—Fascism, Nazism, and Communism. Once these totalitarian movements come to power, the system of terror they establish cannot be overthrown except by war—which every humane person, for obvious reasons, would like to avoid. Liberal and democratic opinion has often proved helpless or inept in meeting the danger. The errors which Kerensky made with regard to the Bolsheviks were repeated by the Weimar Republic with regard to the Nazis. I have discussed elsewhere[9] the cluster of problems connected with the defense of democracy against the varieties of totalitarian attack, but one important problem keeps recurring and deserves extended analysis.

Let us rehearse a few preliminary distinctions in order to determine their bearing on the main problem. One of the great differences between the Fascist and Communist totalitarian movements today is that although both are equally hostile to democratic government, the latter are affiliated with a foreign power and serve as organized fifth columnists of the Kremlin, coödinating their activities at the behest of the Soviet Union with the Communist strategy for world domination.

In the United States, as distinct from some European countries, the Communist movement is not and has never been a domestic danger. It has never even acquired a mass character. But the Communist party and its immediate periphery—consisting of individuals under its discipline, but technically not members—are tied to the international Soviet apparatus in multiple ways. Their chief task is to infiltrate into key sensitive and influential posts in government, trade unions, coöperatives, and peace movements in order to do the bidding of the Kremlin on appropriate occasions. The evidence of this is massive and overwhelming. For this and other reasons, I believe that the Smith Act should be recast or amended, since repeal is impracticable, in order to bring Communist organizational activities, and not its propaganda, under the scope of the law.

This still leaves the chief theoretical question to which I wish to address myself. There are Communists who are quite independent in their notions of how to destroy the open society. They are not affiliated with the Kremlin, and may even be at odds with it on points of sectarian doctrine. There are other types of native totalitarianism, proud of their indigenous character, whose leaders, despite their rhetoric about Americanism, are vehemently opposed to democracy and wish to destroy it. What should the attitude of democrats be toward them if they avoid overt organization and merely teach and preach the necessity for the overthrow of democracy and the establishment of a dictatorship?

The current interpretation of the doctrine of "clear and present danger," referred to in the first chapter, is somewhat vague. I would restate the doctrine in order to make juries, not judges, determiners both of the facts which define the danger and of the specific consequences of the words used. Substantially, this position expresses the point of view of enlightened common sense, as well as the basic Jeffersonian philosophy which is a foe of all absolutism.

It is this Jeffersonian position I wish to contrast with a recurrent view which argues that in principle a democracy is justified in denying political privileges to those who would destroy it. This view has recently been restated with great ingenuity by Professor Ernest van den Haag, and argues that a democracy not merely is justified in repressing groups which *act* or *organize* to overthrow it by violence but is justified in principle in denying the right of political organization to any group that proposes to destroy democracy by peaceful means. The argument runs as follows. Belief in democracy is belief in a system of self-government. This entails the political right and power of its citizens to control and change the government in accordance with their desires. Consequently, the functioning of a democracy is subject to two limitations. Although the citizens may delegate power to the government to rule for a limited period of time, they cannot surrender this power permanently. The government must always return at some point for a renewal of its mandate. Citizens cannot elect to abandon the power of election. Second, the power of the government must be so limited that it cannot deprive citizens of their right to replace it, and cannot suppress those liberties of speech, press, and assembly which are essential to the exercise of that right.

The fathers of our Constitution were successful in protecting us against a government that might keep itself in power by taking away our rights. Less attention was paid to the possibility that some citizens might *give away* their democratic birthright and invite others to do so, as large groups abroad have done. Yet if our right to choose the government freely is *inalienable,* then we are not entitled to *give* the right away any more than the government is entitled to *take* it away. We cannot then elect a government that does not recognize the right of the people to oust it peacefully or that denies the necessary civil liberties. Nor, if freedom is to be inalienable, can invitations to alienate it be recognized as a legitimate part of the democratic process.[10]

This is another way of saying that in a democracy, once it has been established, the one thing that is not open to popular decision is the principle of popular decision itself. Otherwise, so it is claimed, democracy would be self-stultifying. Leonard Nelson, a great German philosopher in the Platonic tradition, came precisely to this conclusion. He argued that democracy was self-defeating because it was based on the self-contradictory principle that all basic policies be decided by majority vote. This made it possible for the majority to vote to abolish majority rule—which is absurd. The argument I am considering denies the contradiction by refusing to allow the use of our political freedom to abolish it. It restricts the application of the majority principle so that the principle itself is not subject to decision. It asserts that one freedom—to give up freedom—must be precluded at *any* time, if freedom is to be preserved at *all* times.

The argument draws an analogy between the freedom of an individual voluntarily to become a slave and the freedom of citizens in a democracy to sacrifice their rights to a dictatorship, and denies the legitimacy of both. Once we abolish involuntary servitude, we cannot permit individuals to alienate their freedom by entering into voluntary servitude. We maximize the amount of desirable freedom in the world by denying them this one freedom. Similarly, once we establish democracy, we cannot permit citizens to alienate their political freedom. In this way, we maximize their freedom of political choice by denying them this one choice. After all, John Stuart Mill himself admitted that the principle of freedom cannot require that a man "should be free not to be free. It is not freedom to be allowed to alienate his freedom."

The argument continues:

. . . by installing a government which is to be the irremovable and total master of their fate, those voting to become *voluntary* political slaves would necessarily compel some of their fellows into *involuntary* servitude. They would not only irreversibly mortgage their own future; they would also deprive of political freedom those who want to keep it. . . .

Nor is this all. Any vote by which we abdicate our right to future free election also robs our children of their heritage of freedom. To allow citizens to vote against democracy is to allow them to sell their children into slavery. . . .

Our heritage permits us forever to elect and to replace governments as we see fit. Our fiduciary duty requires us to keep this sacred trust intact for our children, to protect it against those who want to rob us of it by violence, as well as against those who want to seduce us to give it away. It is not ours to give. Hence, we have no business voting it away and no one has any business trying to corrupt us into doing so. We ought not to permit advocacy of the ballot to extinguish democracy any more than we can allow advocacy of resort to violence. For the end, the surrender of power to a group which would not recognize the right of our children to oust it, is vicious in itself regardless of the means used. And the means are tainted by the vice of the illicit end. To advocate violence to overthrow a democratic government is to propose illegal means for an illegal end. To advocate a vote to overthrow democracy is to advocate an illegal end to be achieved by means that lose their legitimate character to the extent to which they are used for that end.[11]

These arguments express the *absolutist* position on democracy. They make explicit what is implicit in the thought of many conservative critics of democracy. They have considerable weight, but at best, where valid, they add up to an argument *for* retaining democracy, not an argument against permitting *agitation* for the destruction of democracy.

This may be more apparent when we consider some analogous situations. Those who believe in tolerance must, if they are sincere, be opposed to intolerance. To be opposed to intolerance certainly requires that any *acts* of intolerance be prevented or punished; it may even require that incitement to intolerance, when this threatens to eventuate into intolerant action, may be prevented or punished. But does it require that those who propose that our policy of tolerance should be abolished for a policy of intolerance—and give reasons for it—should be prevented or punished for making such proposals? I do not think so. We may condemn them as foolish or even immoral, but we cannot prevent or punish them for making the proposal without abandoning our own principle of tolerance.

Let us concretize this with an example drawn from religious history. Those who believe in religious freedom extend to all religious groups, within the limits of existing moral principles, freedom to practice their religion. In the past some Catholic theologians have asserted that if and when believing Catholics constitute a majority of the population, they would be justified in denying to false and heretical religions the freedom to proselytize as well as their freedom from taxation.

Such action was alleged to be in consonance with their doctrine that it is wrong to permit apostles of false religions to propagate for their faith and thus endanger the eternal salvation of the souls of believers in the true faith. This doctrine had fateful consequences for the Jesuits in Japan in the seventeenth century. The Japanese were, and still are, very tolerant of religious differences. When they discovered that the Jesuits, whom they had previously welcomed, actually believed that Christianity, as they interpreted it, was the only true religion, and that under certain circumstances, this warranted the true believers denying religious freedom to heretics and infidels, they turned on the Jesuits and exterminated them. Religious freedom was only for those who believed in religious freedom.

Today it is denied that this notion of principled intolerance is canonic Catholic doctrine, and some prelates have been excommunicated for professing similar views. But as far as the logic of the situation is concerned, there is no inconsistency in tolerating the expression of all religious opinions including the *opinion,* as distinct from current practice, that the true religious faith justifies in the future repression of religious error. Such an opinion is undoubtedly a powerful reason for not subscribing to such a religion; by itself it is not a sufficient ground for legal interdictment of the profession of the religion. If a group promises some day to interfere with our religious freedom but scrupulously refrains from doing so now, our duty is to agitate and educate to prevent them from winning political power to carry out their threat to our religious freedom. It is not to violate their religious freedom now.

Is the situation any different with respect to belief in democracy? Must a democracy make the democratic principle an unchallengeable axiom in political thought? The faith of democracy rests upon the belief that the interests which divide men may be more successfully settled to their mutual satisfaction by popular debate, discussion, and the give and take of peaceful negotiation than by anarchy or despotism. Shall this faith itself be made sacrosanct, immune to critical inquiry? Shall we, in the name of democracy, refuse to permit democracy to be judged for fear of losing it forever? Grant that the fear and danger are there. Is the only way of meeting it the conversion of a democratic principle into an absolute presupposition? If it is, in what way does a democracy of this sort logically differ from a form of despotism—however enlightened or benevolent? We are told that "when necessary we must restrict the people's rule to conserve their liberty." Is this not equivalent to abandoning the majority principle and substituting the rule of the watchful minority who must set themselves up as the perpetual guardians of the liberties of their wards—the people? Politically, this reformulates the position of Rousseau that, if necessary, individuals and, for that matter, the entire people, since numbers are irrelevant here, must be "forced to be free"—the premise or seed of a new authoritarianism.

Is it permissible for a majority to alienate the freedom of a minority together with its own? No, not if one believes in freedom. But if the majority does not believe in freedom, even though as a minority we may fiercely complain and forcibly resist it, we cannot charge it with inconsistency. If the majority does believe in freedom, and prevents the minority which wishes to alienate its own and others' freedom from doing so, the minority in this instance has the same formal right to complaint and can take the same risk of action. There is no logical inconsistency here either.

Every majority decision in a democracy decides something, good or bad, to which by definition the minority is opposed. But we are not discussing what is specifically good or bad, but only the legitimacy of the majority action, under the democratic rules, in voting into office those who will destroy democracy. If a democracy behaves this way, it would establish, for those who believe in personal freedom, sufficient evidence of the inadequacy of a democratic system to preserve human freedom and a decent social order. It does not justify them in asserting that a true democracy consists in preventing the majority from doing what is foolish or unwise. If this were to be construed as democracy, we should have to regard Plato as a democrat-something, which would be dismissed as absurd in the light of customary usage.

The same considerations hold in considering the argument that the surrender of democracy by any majority is "undemocratic" because it binds future generations. No decision irrevocably binds future generations. The decision to uphold a democratic system does not obligate future generations to preserve it; the decision to surrender it does not prevent future generations from restoring it. ?

Any political system which accepts the premise that a people must be forced to be free seems to me to be psychologically defective. Freedom—like loyalty, like love—by the very nature of the human emotions involved, cannot be commanded. Those who are prevented from expressing their wish to challenge democracy will not thereby cease wishing and feeling. They will be driven to express their determination to transform the system of democracy by hypocritical professions of strengthening it.

Despite asseverations to the contrary, the danger that a people which has once enjoyed democracy will voluntarily vote a totalitarian regime into power, although always present, seen in the perspective of history has rarely been acute. Historically, there is no clear example in which the majority of a self-governing people entrusted its destiny to a dictator who declared that he would end their liberties in the future. Neither Bolshevism nor Fascism came to power through the vicissitudes of the free political process. Although Hitler reached the chancellorship by constitutional means, the Nazi party received a majority only after a campaign in which it unloosened a reign of terror against its political opponents. Nonetheless, instances can be cited of communities living in comparative freedom which voluntarily voted to place themselves under the heel of dictatorships. The plebiscite by which the Saar voted to rejoin a Nazi Germany rather than affiliate with a democratic France or remain independent shows that the spirit of nationalism may be stronger than allegiance to democracy. Today in Italy and France a complex pattern of fear, hate, and myth may prove stronger than both the spirit of nationalism and the love of freedom. Although improbable, the situation is not inconceivable.

Nonetheless, it is not necessary to make a religious absolute out of any set of political institutions and place them beyond the reach of criticism and change. The greatness, the nobility of the American Revolution lies in the fact that it was conceived as an experiment in liberty. Until the thought of the American Enlightenment challenged the view, it was assumed, on the basis of the record of human ignorance, folly, and cruelty in history, that men were born either to rule or to be ruled. It was the daring hypothesis of the philosopher-statesmen of the American Republic that if given an opportunity, under conditions in which they had free access to information and in which traditions of free speech and press prevailed, men could be trusted to govern themselves. "I have no fear," wrote Jefferson, "but that the result of our experiment will be, that men may be trusted to govern themselves without a master. Could the contrary of this be proved, I should conclude either that there is no God, or that He is a malevolent being." [12]

Events have so far confirmed this faith, although it has come near to failing. But it cannot be finally confirmed, because self-government is a *continuing experiment* facing new challenges which are created by the very successes of the past, challenges which require more and more resourcefulness, more and better education, and a commitment as deep and sustained as that which inspired those who left us our heritage of freedom.

Jefferson and those who fought to make the American experiment in freedom succeed staked not only their faith in God and human intelligence, they staked their very lives. Creative intelligence, courage to think and act on a world scale, and a passion for human freedom cannot guarantee the survival of liberal civilization today, but they are our best hope.

The world we live in is far removed from Jefferson's. The dangers to peace and to freedom are more massive and dreadful than he ever conceived them. Only those who refuse to

see can deny that the threatening tides of Communist totalitarianism threaten to engulf the remaining islands of freedom
—West Berlin, West Germany, Western Europe. They are
already lapping at the shores of the Western Hemisphere, not
far from the North American mainland. The prospects of
conflict are so fearful that one can observe in Europe and in
Great Britain, and even in the United States, a growing mood
which defines our choice as limited to universal destruction,
if we resist Communist aggression, or surrender to Communism if we do not resist. These alternatives are neither exclusive nor exhaustive—not exclusive, because surrender does
not guarantee survival; not exhaustive, because there is an
entire gamut of possibilities that remain to be explored
which, without sacrificing human freedom, can preserve
peace.

In moments of crisis, however, there are those who are prepared to abandon the experiment of freedom and self-government for the sake of survival at any price and at all costs in
human infamy. They say that if the defense of freedom imperils peace, then better life under Communist despotism,
with all its evils, than the risk of destruction. To which, I
reply, invoking in all humility the values of the Jeffersonian
tradition: Those who will never risk their lives for freedom
will surely lose their freedom without surely saving their
lives; that unless we prize something in life which is more
precious than mere life, we have renounced the human estate,
that in our precarious world, intelligence and courage have
proved to have greater survival value than hysterical fear;
and that if we continue to place our trust in them, we are
justified, in Jefferson's words, "to disdain despair, encourage
trial, and nourish hope."

Notes

CHAPTER 1

1. Letter to Thomas Law, June 13, 1814, *The Life and Selected Writings of Thomas Jefferson*, edited by Koch and Peden (New York: Random House, 1944), p. 638.
2. Letter to Danbury Baptist Association, January 1, 1802, *ibid.*, p. 332.
3. Letter to Peter Carr, August 10, 1787, *ibid.*, p. 430.
4. Opinion as Secretary of State, April 28, 1793, *ibid.*, p. 319.
5. *The Living Thoughts of Thomas Jefferson*, edited by John Dewey (New York: Longmans, Green), 1940, p. 91.
6. Letter to F. A. Vander Kemp, March 22, 1812, Koch and Peden, *op. cit.*, p. 618.
7. Letter to Thomas Law, June 13, 1814, *ibid.*, p. 639.
8. Dewey, *op. cit.*, Introduction, p. 24.
9. *Everyman Edition* (New York: Dutton), Vol. 2, p. 242.
10. *Ibid.*, p. 252.
11. *Works*, edited by John Bowring (Edinburgh, 1839), Vol. 2, p. 501.
12. *Ibid.*, p. 497.
13. *Theory of Legislation*, edited by C. Ogden (New York: Harcourt, Brace, 1931), p. 94.
14. Rudolf Allers, in *Freedom and Authority in Our Times*, edited by Bryson and Finkelstein (New York: Harpers, 1950), p. 570.
15. *Op. cit.*, pp. 94–95.
16. Hans J. Morgenthau, *The American Political Science Review* (September, 1957), p. 714. After the criticism of this passage was written, I found the same point made in Felix Oppenheim, *Dimensions of Freedom* (New York: St. Martin's Press, 1961), pp. 129–130.
17. "The Bill of Rights," 35, New York University Law Review 867 (1960).
18. *Political Freedom* (New York: Harpers, 1960), p. 20.
19. Letter to J. B. Colvin, September 20, 1810, Koch and Peden, *op. cit.*, pp. 606–607.
20. *Harpers Magazine* (February, 1961).
21. *Korematsu* v. *U.S.* 214 (1944). The opinion for the majority of six judges found "pressing public necessity" for the evacuation of the Japanese.
22. Quoted by Zechariah Chafee, "Three Evils in American Destiny," *The Christian Unitarian Register*, May, 1952, p. 14.
23. For decision upholding the outlawing of polygamy, *Reynolds* v. *U.S.*, 98 U.S. 145 (1878); compelling vaccination against smallpox, *Jacobson* v. *Mass.*, 197 U.S. 11 (1905); prohibiting the handling of poisonous snakes in religious ceremony, *State* v. *Bunn*, 229 N.C. 734 (1949), appeal from which dismissed, 336 U.S. 942 (1949); compelling education of children against religious objection, *Peco* v. *Donner*, 302 N.Y. 857 (1951), appeal from which dismissed, 342 U.S. 884 (1951); justifying tax on religious litera-

ture, if not discriminatory, *Watchtower Bible and Tract Soc.* v. *Los Angeles*, 181 F. 2d 739 (1950); certiori denied 340 U.S. 820 (1950).

24. John Neville Figgis, *Studies of Political Thought from Gerson to Gratius 1414–1625*, Cambridge University Press, Second edition, 1956 reprint, p. 118.

25. 35 *New York University Law Review*, 873–4 (1960).

26. These words of Mr. Justice Black are not part of an actual opinion but of an hypothetical case considered by him in the article cited above in which he attempts to show the dire results which would ensue if the Court adopted a "balancing approach" to conflict of rights. In discussing the plaintiff's case, which the hypothetical decision of the hypothetical Court wrongfully rejects according to Justice Black, the Court says: "The Plaintiff contends that the Fifth Amendment's provision about compensation is so absolute a command that Congress is wholly without authority to violate it, however great the nation's emergency and peril may be." This is obviously Justice Black's contention, too, for he identifies himself completely with the case of the plaintiff. Presumably the bar against the action of Congress is also a bar against the action of the Chief Executive.

27. *Ibid.*, p. 877.

28. *Ibid.*, p. 878.

29. *Mugler* v. *Kansas*, 123 U.S. 622 (1887); *Hawes* v. *Ga.* 258 U.S. 1 (1922).

30. *Miller* v. *Schoene*, 276 U.S. 272 (1928).

31. *Beauharnais* v. *Illinois*, 343 U.S. 250 (1951).

32. Leonard W. Levy, *Legacy of Suppression: Freedom of Speech and Press in Early American History* (Cambridge, Mass.: Harvard University Press, 1960). The author summarizes his findings in the Preface.

> "I find that libertarian theory from the time of Milton to the ratification of the First Amendment substantially accepted the right of the state to suppress seditious libel. I find also that the American experience with freedom of political expression was as slight as the theoretical inheritance was narrow. Indeed, the American legislatures, especially during the colonial period, were far more oppressive than the supposedly tyrannous common law courts. The evidence drawn particularly from the period 1776 to 1791 indicates that the generation that framed the first state declarations of rights and the First Amendment was hardly as libertarian as we have traditionally assumed. They did not intend to give free rein to criticism of the government that might be deemed to be seditious libel, although the concept of seditious libel was—and still is the principal basis of muzzling political dissent. There is even reason to believe that the Bill of Rights was more the chance product of political expediency on all sides than of principled commitment to personal liberties. A broad libertarian theory of freedom of speech and press did not emerge in the United States until the Jeffersonians, when a minority party, were forced to defend themselves against the Alien and Sedition Acts of 1798. In power, however, the Jeffersonians were not much more tolerant of their political critics than the Federalists had been." Pp. vii–viii (quoted with permission).

33. *Ibid.*, p. 879.

34. *Beauharnais* v. *Ill.*, 343 U.S. 250 (1952).

35. 28 *Harvard Law Review*, 343 (1915).

36. Letter to James Madison, July 31, 1788, Koch and Peden, *op. cit.*, p. 451.
37. *Frowerk* v. *United States*, 249 U.S. 208 (1919) [italics added].
38. *Schenck* v. *United States*, 249 U.S. 47 (1919).
39. Milton R. Konvitz, *Fundamental Liberties of a Free People* (Ithaca: Cornell University Press, 1957), p. 307.
40. *Whitney* v. *California*, 274 U.S. 357 (1927).
41. *Minersville* v. *Gobitis*, 310 U.S. 586 (1940); *W. Va.* v. *Barnette*, 319 U.S. 624 (1943).
42. 354 U.S. 340 (1957) [emphasis supplied]. Of this sentence, Professor Malcolm Sharp writes in his foreword to the second edition of A. Meiklejohn's *Political Freedom* (New York: Harper), p. xx: "Indeed, in view of the ambiguity of the word 'incites' in its application to various circumstances, it may be that Mr. Justice Black is going further in protecting freedom of speech than Mr. Meiklejohn, in conversation, has indicated he would be ready to go." The obvious fact is that the word "incitement" is not very ambiguous. The range of its meanings, as given by Webster's Unabridged New International Dictionary, extends as follows: "to move to action; to stir up or urge on; as, to *incite* a mob to action." In every sense of incitement here listed, to incite to a criminal act is legally punishable.

    As far as the text of Meiklejohn's own writing goes, there is a curious ambiguity in his definition of "incitement." He writes: "An incitement, I take it, is an utterance so related to a specific overt act that it may be regarded as treated as a part of the doing of the act itself, *if the act is done. (Op. cit.,* p. 123, italics added.) If this means that the specific overt act must be carried out or actually attempted before words may be considered an incitement, Meiklejohn's position does not differ from that of Justice Black. On this view, no one can be taxed with inciting to riot or lynching until the riot or lynching actually begins. If Professor Sharp's report is correct, perhaps the italicized phrase was intended to read, "were the act to be done."
43. Cf. by "The Illogic of Mr. Justice Black," *New Leader*, December 2, 1957.
44. *Rockwell* v. *Morris*, 7 L. Ed (U.S.) 131 (1961).
45. *Political Freedom,* The Constitutional Powers of the People (New York: Harper, 1960), p. 21.
46. *Ibid.*, p. 57.
47. *Ibid.*, p. 112.
48. Cf. *ibid., passim*, especially Chapter iii. Typical pronouncements, combined with an expression of admiration for Holmes's style and personality: "Mr. Holmes . . . flatly repudiates the moral compact on which our plan of government rests. And, especially, he breaks down the basic principle of the First Amendment." (p. 70). Similarly, on Frankfurter, (p. 101). And on the Court to the extent that it has followed Holmes, ". . . today I would say . . . that the Supreme Court of the last forty years [i.e., since the formulation by Holmes of the doctrine of clear and present danger], more than any other agency or person in our society, must be held responsible for the destruction of these Constitutional principles which that court is commissioned to interpret and to defend" (p. 106).
49. *Ibid.*, p. 86.
50. *Ibid.*, p. 87.

51. Ernest Nagel, *Logic Without Metaphysics* (Glencoe: The Free Press, 1956), pp. 401 ff. Cf. also my *Education for Modern Man* (New York, Dial Press, 1946), pp. 41 ff.

52. *The Individual, the State and World Government* (New York: Macmillan, 1947), p. 35.

53. Justices Black and Douglas have contributed heavily to this literature of woe and lamentation without being deterred or sobered in the slightest by the failure of the calamitous events they predicted to come to pass. Writing about the New York State Feinberg Law, a foolish and unnecessary piece of legislation which requires Superintendents of Schools to report on whether teachers are members of the Communist Party, Justice Douglas delivered himself of the following predictions:

> "The very threat of such a procedure is certain to raise havoc with academic freedom. Youthful indiscretions, mistaken causes, misguided enthusiasms—all long forgotten—become the ghosts of a harrowing present. Any organization committed to a liberal cause, any group organized to revolt against an hysterical trend, any committee launched to sponsor an unpopular program becomes suspect.
>
> "The law inevitably turns the school system into a spying project. Regular loyalty reports on the teachers must be made out. The principals become detectives; the students, the parents, the community become informers . . .
>
> "What happens under this law is typical of what happens in a police state. Teachers are under constant surveillance; their pasts are combed for signs of disloyalty; their utterances are watched for clues to dangerous thoughts. A pall is cast over the classrooms . . ."

> "Supineness and dogmatism take the place of inquiry. A 'party line'—as dangerous as the 'party line' of the Communists—lays hold. Fear stalks the classroom. . . ." *Adler* v. *Board of Education*, 342 U.S. 498 (1952). And more in this vein. Ten years have elapsed since the Feinberg Law was put into operation. The horrendous picture drawn by Justice Douglas has proved to be false in every particular. Irrespective of the merits of the law, this prediction has been shown by the evidence of the events to have been hysterical in tone and content.

54. 35 *New York University Law Review* 878 [emphasis mine].

55. *Perez* v. *Brownell*, 356 U.S. 44 (1958) .

56. *Op. cit.*, p. 879.

57. *The Living Thoughts of Thomas Jefferson*, Dewey edition, *op. cit.*, p. 54.

58. *Ibid.*, p. 130.

59. *Perez* v. *Brownell*, 356 U.S. 81 (1958).

60. *The Papers of Thomas Jefferson*, Boyd edition, Vol. 13, p. 44 (1956). In this letter to Madison, Jefferson argues for the inclusion of a Bill of Rights to the Constitution.

61. *Adventures of Ideas* (New York: Macmillan, 1935), p. 502. In this connection see the illuminating essay by Milton Konvitz on "Dewey and Jefferson" in *John Dewey—Philosopher of Science and Freedom*, edited by S. Hook (New York: Dial, 1949).

62. Morris R. Cohen, *The Faith of a Liberal* (New York: Harcourt, Brace).

63. *Notes on the State of Virginia,* edited with an Introduction and notes by William Peden (Chapel Hill: University of North Carolina Press, 1955), p. 165.
64. Eugene V. Rostow, *Notre Dame Lawyer* (August, 1958), p. 577.

CHAPTER 2

1. *Life of John Marshall* (Boston, 1919), Vol. III, p. 11.
2. Letter to Peter Carr, *The Living Thoughts of Jefferson,* edited by John Dewey (New York: Longmans, Green, 1940), p. 84.
3. Charles L. Black, Jr., *The People and the Court,* New York: 1960, p. 52.

    ". . . I have described the function of the Supreme Court in a way which turns the usual account upside down. The role of the Court has usually been conceived as that of *invalidating* 'hasty' or 'unwise' legislation, of acting as a 'check' on the other departments . . . But a case can be made for believing that the prime and most necessary function of the Court has been that of *validation,* not that of invalidation. What a government of limited power needs, at the beginning and forever, is some means of satisfying the people that it has taken all the steps humanly possible to stay within its powers. That is the condition of its legitimacy, and its legitimacy, in the long run, is the condition of its life. And the Court, through its history, has acted as the legitimator of the government. In a very real sense, the Government of the United States is based on the opinions of the Supreme Court."

    If this were true one would be justified in saying that in a very real sense, the Supreme Court *is* the Government of the United States and not one of its coordinate branches.
4. Quoted by Bernard Schwartz, *The Supreme Court: Constitutional Revolution in Retrospect* (New York: The Ronald Press, 1957), p. 4. Justice Hughes goes so far as to assert that this is true of every law.

    "The labors of the Supreme Court in applying general clauses of an undefined content are not limited to the duty of giving effect to the Constitution. The Court is the final interpreter of the acts of Congress. Statutes come to the judicial test not simply of constitutional validity but with respect to their true import, and a federal stature finally means what the Court says it means."

    The Supreme Court of the United States (New York: Columbia University Press, 1928), p. 230. Presumably this is true, even if it is the precise opposite of what Congress meant or what a sober and scholarly analysis of the language of the text shows the meaning to be.
5. *United States* v. *Butler,* 297 U.S. 1, 78–9 (1936).
6. *Of Law and Men* (New York: 1957), p. 17.
7. *The Supreme Court in the American System of Government* (Cambridge, Mass.: Harvard University Press, 1955), p. 58.
8. *Osborn* v. *Bank of the United States,* 9 Wheaton's Reports (22 U.S.) 738 at 866 (1824).
9. *The Common Law* (Boston: Little, Brown, 1881), pp. 1, 35.
10. *Opus cited,* 4 supra, p. 24.
11. The first was written June 2, 1807; the second June 11, 1815, *The Writings of Thomas Jefferson,* edited by Paul Leicester Ford, Vol. IX, pp. 53–

Notes

54 and 517–519. In another letter to William Jarvis, September 28, 1820 (*op. cit.* Vol. X, pp. 160–161), Jefferson not only reaffirms his early view but denies in emphatic words the contrary view. "You seem . . . to consider the judges as the ultimate arbiters of all constitutional questions; a very dangerous doctrine, indeed, and one which would place us under the despotism of an oligarchy."

12. *Ibid.*, letter to William Jarvis.
13. Beveridge, A., *Life of John Marshall*, Vol. III, p. 177.
14. *Ibid.*
15. Ford, *The Writings of Thomas Jefferson*, I, pp. 111–114.
16. Charles L. Black, Jr., *The People and the Courts*, p. 186.
17. *Ex parte McCardle*, 7 Wall. 506 (1868).
18. *Scott v. Sanford*, 19 How. 393 (1857).
19. See the highly significant testimony of Joseph L. Rauh, *Hearings before the Subcommittee of the Committee on the Judiciary United States Senate on Limitation of Appellate Jurisdiction of the United States Supreme Court, 85th Congress, Second Session,* on S. 2646, February 19–21, 1958, p. 65 (Washington: United States Government Printing Office, 1958). See also along the same lines the testimony of Leonard B. Boudin, p. 635. This entire volume will repay study as indicating the attitude of the legal profession as a whole to the latest attempt made to limit the appellate jurisdiction of the Court.
20. *Supra,* p. 366.
21. Charles A. Horsky, 42 *Minnesota Law Review* 1111 (1957–8)—this is a not untypical expression found in many of the law journals of the year.
22. *Supra*, note 15 at 368.
23. *Osborn v. Bank of the United States,* see footnote 7 *supra.*
24. *New Leader,* May 30, 1936, Vol. 19, p. 5 [italics in original].
25. Cf. my *Common Sense and the Fifth Amendment* (New York: Criterion Books, 1957).
26. Cf. Alpheus T. Mason, *Harlan Fiske Stone: Pillar of the Law* (New York: Viking Press, 1956), pp. 628–647.
27. *The People and the Courts,* pp. 180–181.
28. 7 *Harvard Law Review* (1893) at 154–5 [my italics].
29. *We, the Judges,* 1956, N.Y., p. 445.
30. *Miss., Kansas and Texas v. May,* 194 U.S. 267. Chafee somewhere comments sourly on Holmes's observation by pointing out that legislatures unfortunately do not remember this but have to be reminded of it by the courts. The obvious rejoinder to Chafee's comment is that with respect to the people's *welfare* it is palpably false. With respect to the people's *liberties,* to the extent it is true, it may very well be the presumptuous claim by the Court that it alone is the guardian of the people's liberties which accounts for slackness in the legislative guardianship. For it may be that the legislature has come to believe it and therefore not properly exercised its constitutional responsibility. Before the Court acquired its full blown powers, Constitutional questions were much more vigorously debated in Congress.
31. *Youngstown Sheet and Tube Co. v. Sawyer,* 343 U.S. 579 (1952).
32. Frankfurter, Felix, *Mr. Justice Holmes and the Supreme Court* (Cambridge: Harvard University Press, 1938), pp. 50–51.

Notes

33. *U.S.* v. *Rabinowitz*, 339 U.S. at 86 (1950).
34. I refer here to *U.S.* v. *Lovett*, 328 U.S. 303 (1946) in which Congress foolishly sought to cut off funds for the payment of the services of three officials who had a record of past affiliation with Communist front organizations. The Senate and the President were strongly opposed to the legislation and yielded to House stubbornness unnecessarily. The action of the Congress did not prevent the three men affected from working for the government but refused to authorize payment.

   An interesting review of decisions which nullified Congressional actions through 1943 will be found in Commager, Henry, *Majority Rule and Minority Rights* (New York: Oxford University Press, 1943), pp. 47–56. His conclusions are extremely critical of the claims made for the Court as a protector of minority rights.

   A recent case, *Trop* v. *Dulles*, 385 U.S. 86 (1958), which is sometimes cited as another instance of valiant defense of individual liberty against oppressive action of the Congress, seems to me to be a flagrant illustration of judicial usurpation of the legislative function. The opinion is puzzling in its logic and questionable to common sense. By a vote of 5 to 4, the Court decided that Congress has no right to deprive an individual of his citizenship who has been found guilty of desertion in war time and thereupon dishonorably discharged from the military service. The majority opinion contends that the right of citizenship, once acquired, is absolute and inalienable. Citizenship may be voluntarily renounced but in no circumstances can Congress alienate it. It is admitted, however, that certain words and actions may be evidence of such voluntary renunciation even though the individual in question may deny that he thereby intends to renounce his citizenship.

   The opinion also admits that Congress may prescribe the conditions under which conduct may be taken as evidence of voluntary renunciation of allegiance. The Court, however, refuses to regard desertion in war time, after this has been established by due process and followed by dishonorable discharge, as at least as reasonable an indication of renunciation of citizenship, as marriage to an alien which the opinion holds to be evidence of voluntary expatriation while the marriage lasts, despite the obvious fact that this may very well have been the last thing in the mind of a woman who married an alien. The view that citizenship is an inalienable right but that Congress may prescribe, with the permission of the Court, the conditions under which it may legitimately be inferred that citizenship has been voluntarily alienated, independently of the *intentions* of the individual, is radically incoherent. To argue further, as the opinion does, that denationalization is a cruel and unusual punishment for desertion in war time, an action for which death is a very widely recognized and approved penalty, is not an intelligent expression of civil libertarianism against Congressional violation of Constitutional freedoms but sentimentalism supported by dubious inference.

35. *The Nature of the Judicial Process*, 1921, p. 94.
36. The following opinion by a contemporary figure, who may be considered a moderate, reflects the judgment of the vast segment of the American people at the time who were neither Abolitionists nor Southern hotheads:

   "The course of the majority of judges in this case of Dred Scott precipitated the action of causes which produced our civil war, and which otherwise would have lain dormant until the period of danger to the Union, arising out of the existence of slavery, had passed by. If, without such an excitement as was occasioned by what was claimed to have been the 'decision' of the Supreme Court on the subject of slavery in the Territories, we could have gained ten years more in the growth of the North and in the peaceful development of the power of the Federal government within the just limits of the Constitution, Southern secession would never have been attempted. On the one hand, without the stimulus afforded by this 'decision,' there would have been no adequate cause for the formation in the Northern states of a geographical party, with professed efforts aimed at the supposed predominance of the 'slave-power' in the councils of the nation. On the other hand, without the new and unnecessary stimulus of this supposed 'decision,' Southern feeling in regard to the importance of a theoretical right to carry slaves into the Territories must have died a natural death. It could not have risen to a sense of danger to their equality in the Union, merely because the people of the North were unwilling to see the area of slavery extended through the Territories. It was the factitious importance given to the supposed constitutional right of such extension, by the venerable persons composing the majority of the Supreme Court, that awakened anew a jealousy which had already subsided under the tranquilizing influence of the great settlement made seven years before."

The Life and Writings of B. R. Curtis. A Memoir by George Ticknor Curtis edited by B. R. Curtis, Jr. (Boston: Little, Brown, 1879), Vol. I, pp. 195-6. George Ticknor Curtis was the brother of Supreme Court Justice Curtis who wrote the dissenting opinion in the Dred Scott case.

37. *Plessy v. Ferguson,* 163 U.S. 537 (1896).
38. *Brown v. Board of Education of Topeka,* 347 U.S. 483 (1954).
39. *Dennis v. United States,* 341 U.S. 494 (1951).
40. *Yates v. United States,* 354 U.S. 298 (1957).
41. *Muller v. Oregon,* 208 U.S. 419 (1908) on the occasion of the so-called Brandeis brief. This dictum is honored more in the breach than in the observance, especially by the absolutist school of judicial activists.
42. Wechsler, Herbert, *Principles, Politics and Fundamental Law* (Cambridge, Mass.: Harvard University Press, 1961), p. 27.
43. *An Introduction to the Study of the Law of the English Constitution,* 10th edition (London, 1960), with an introduction by E. C. S. Wade, p. 175.
44. *The Life and Selected Writings of Thomas Jefferson,* edited by Koch and Peden (New York: Random House, 1944), p. 324.
45. Beveridge, *Life of Marshall,* Vol. III, p. 61. Hamilton has been credited with the remark "The people, Sir—the people is a great beast" by Allen Nevins in the *Dictionary of American Biography,* VIII, p. 179, but I have been unable to track down the source of the remark even with the help of my colleagues among the historians. But the sentiment of disdain for the people is so characteristic of Hamilton's other writings that it is no injustice to attribute the sense of the alleged utterance to him—for example, "Take mankind in general, they are vicious, their passions may be operated upon," Hamilton, *Works* (1904), I, 408. I am indebted

to Professor William Leuchtenberg of Columbia University for this and similar references to Hamilton's regard for his fellow citizens.

46. Brogan, D. W., *Government of the People: A Study in the American Political System,* p. 36.
47. *Ibid.,* p. 246.
48. "The Firstness of the First Amendment," 65 *The Yale Law Journal* at 480 (1955–6).
49. *The Bill of Rights* (Cambridge, Mass.: Harvard University Press, 1958), *passim.*
50. *Ibid.,* p. 67.

CHAPTER 3

1. *Federal Reporter,* Second Series, 183, F2d at 213 (1950).
2. See the interesting account of the events and the spirit of the times in Massachusetts during the 1850's. *The Life and Writings of B. R. Curtis: A Memoir by George Tichnor Curtis,* edited by B. R. Curtis, Jr. (Boston: Little, Brown, 1879), Vol. I.
3. *The Collected Works of Abraham Lincoln* (Basler edition), Vol. I, p. 112. (New Brunswick: Rutgers University Press, 1953.) Lincoln's speech was delivered in 1838. In this connection, it is pertinent to observe that Jefferson in listing the essential principles of the American government emphasizes "absolute acquiescence in the decisions of the majority—the vital principle of republics, from which there is no appeal but to force, the vital principle and immediate parent of despotism." "First Inaugural Address," March 4, 1801. Commager, H *Documents of American History,* Vol. I, p. 188.
4. Quoted by Curtis, *op. cit.,* Vol. I, p. 127.
5. *Yale Review* (Spring, 1961), p. 463.
6. *Ibid.,* p. 478.
7. *The History of Freedom and Other Essays,* edited by Lawrence and Figgis (London, 1907), p. 3.
8. E. M. Forster, *Two Cheers for Democracy* (New York: Harcourt, Brace, 1951), p. 78.
9. Cf. my *Heresy, Yes—Conspiracy, No* (New York: John Day, 1953) and *Political Power and Personal Freedom* (New York: Criterion Books, 1959).
10. The argument is presented in two places, *The Fabric of Society* by Ernest van den Haag and Ralph Ross (New York: Harcourt, Brace, 1958), pp. 632 ff. and in "Controlling Subversive Groups" by Van den Haag, *The Annals of the American Academy of Political and Social Science* (July, 1955), pp. 62 ff. The quotations in the text are from the latter, with the permission of the author.
11. *Ibid.,* pp. 63–65.
12. Letter of July 2, 1787, *The Living Thoughts of Thomas Jefferson,* presented by John Dewey (New York: Longmans, Green, 1940), p. 67.

Index

abolitionists, 114
absolutism (absolute), 14–31 *passim*, 39–42, 46–47, 51–53, 96, 105, 114, 134
abuse of power, 59
Acton, Lord, 127
advocacy. *See* incitement
Africa, 2
Aldermaston marchers, 107
Algeria, 107
Alien and Sedition Laws, 94
Amendments:
  First, 15, 22, 25–38 *passim*, 40–45, 53, 94, 101, 102
  Fifth, 26–29, 40–43, 53, 80, 119
  Sixth, 53
  Eleventh, 69, 79
  Fourteenth, 28, 79, 87
  Eighteenth, 28, 115
American Revolution, 3, 9, 31, 138
anarchists, 42
Antigone, 108
apriorism, 42
Aquinas, Thomas, 83
Aristotle, 111
Autobiography (Jefferson), 74

"balancing approach," 53, 55
Bentham, Jeremy, 8–10
Beveridge, Albert, 73, 102
Bill of Rights, 14, 15, 17, 21–32 *passim*, 39, 40, 44, 51–57 *passim*, 86, 87, 92, 97, 98, 114
Black, Charles L., 18, 144 n. 3
Black, Justice Hugo L., 14, 18, 19, 22, 25–31, 37, 38, 48, 50, 143 n. 53
Bolsheviks, 130, 137
Boston, 114
Brandeis, Justice Louis D., 21, 34–35
Brown, John, 20, 117, 123

Brown v. *Board of Education*, 93
Burr's trial, 71

Cahan, Edmund, 99
Caligula, 84
cannibalism, 36
Cardozo, Benjamin N., 21, 91, 92
Casper, 39
Catholics, 28, 134–135
censorship. *See* Amendment, First
Chase, Justice Salmon P., 73, 102
Chiaromonte, Nicola, 122
China, 50
civil disobedience, 107, 120, 124–126
civil liberties, 88, 91, 99, 100, 132
Civil Rights Act (1875), 92
Civil War, 92, 104, 111
"clear and present danger," 33–34, 44
Cohen, Morris R., 58, 79
Colvin, J. B., 18
The Common Law (Holmes), 69
Communists (communism), 23, 39, 43, 52, 58, 93, 109, 110, 125, 126, 130, 131, 139
Corwin, Edward S., 74
Court Room Reform Bill (1937), 81
Creon, 108
Crito (Plato), 118
"cruel and unusual punishment," 54
Curtis, Justice Benjamin R., 116

Daughters of the American Revolution, 31
Declaration concerning the Right of Insubordination (1960). *See* Declaration of the 121
Declaration of Independence, 7, 9, 14, 109, 111
Declaration of the 121: 107, 111, 122
Declaration of the Rights of Man, 8

149

Index

Labour government, 107
Laissez faire, 60, 88
Law, Thomas, 5
Lenin, 84
Lincoln, 12, 28, 29, 33, 64, 114, 116, 118, 126
Locke, John, 7
lynching, 37, 38

McCardle case, 76–77
Madison, James, 33, 35, 89, 92
Marbury v. *Madison*, 71, 76, 82
Marcus Aurelius, 84
Marshal, Justice John, 63, 69, 71, 73, 77, 79, 97, 102, 104
Marx, 89
Massachusetts, 114, 116
Meiklejohn, Alexander, 15, 39–45
Mill, John Stuart, 133
morality, 16, 17
More, Sir Thomas, 20
Morgenthau, Hans J. (cited), 12
Mormons, 24–25
Morris, Gouverneur, 97
Muslims, 23
Muste, A. J., 119

Nagel, Ernest, 45
nationalism, 137, 138
natural rights. *See* human rights
Nazism, 125, 130, 137
Negroes, 39, 79, 92, 93, 108
Nelson, Leonard, 132
New Deal, 61
nuclear armament, 107

O'Brian, John Lord, 77
Old Testament, 24

Parker, Theodore, 116
Parliament (British), 23, 87, 98, 102
Pinkney, William, 63
Plato, 45, 65, 96, 105, 132, 136
plural marriages, 24–25
pogrom, 37
Poland (Poles), 10
polygamy, 24–25
pope, 82
Popper, Karl, 58
Pound, Roscoe, 32, 77

press. *See* Amendment, First
Proclamation of Emancipation, 28–29
prohibition. *See* Amendment, Eighteenth
property rights, 89
public affairs, 38–42
public welfare, 46, 51
Putsch, 109, 110

Quisling, 129

radio, 44
"reasons of state," 55
Rechtsphilosophie (Hegel), 88
Reconstruction, 80
Reform Laws, 98
Registration Act, 119
Reith Lectures, 50
religion, 23–25, 46, 128, 135
Renan, Ernest, 111
Republic (Plato), 105
revolution, 106–139 *passim*
Rockwell, 39
Roosevelt, Franklin D., 80–81
Ross, Sir William, 16
Rousseau, 45, 136
Russell, Bertrand, 107, 123

Saar, 137
"safety of the people," 53
Santayana, George, 105
Sartre, Jean-Paul, 107, 120
Schenck case, 35
Schwartz, Bernard (cited), 144 n. 4
Scott v. *Sanford*, 77, 82, 92, 100, 116
"separation of powers," 100
Sharp, Malcolm (cited), 142 n. 42
sit-ins, 125
slavery, 28, 114, 116, 133
"slippery slope" argument, 47–50
Smith Act, 93, 94
Social Statics (Spencer), 88
Socrates, 118
South America, 2, 109
Spanish Loyalists, 122
Spencer, Herbert, 88
Stalin, 20, 65, 84
Steel Seizure case, 86
Stone, Chief Justice Harlan F., 67

Index